CHINADA:
Memoirs of the Gang of Seven

Gary Geddes
Robert Kroetsch
Adele Wiseman
Patrick Lane
Alice Munro
Suzanne Paradis
Geoffrey Hancock

QUADRANT EDITIONS

Copyright © the authors, 1982

Published by Quadrant Editions, RR No. 1, Dunvegan, Ontario, K0C 1J0
Distribution: c/o English Department, Concordia University,
1455 de Maisonneuve Blvd. West,
Montreal, Quebec, H3G 1M8

Typeset by Adcomp in Montreal and
printed by Hignell in Winnipeg,
December 1982.

Calligraphy by Ng Wan Fung.

Photographs by Gary Geddes and Geoff Hancock.

ISBN 0-86495-019-5

CONTENTS

PREFACE

On June 29, 1981 a very motley and unusual group of Canadian writers, consisting of Adele Wiseman, Suzanne Paradis, Alice Munro, Patrick Lane, Robert Kroetsch, Geoff Hancock, and myself, left for a historic visit to the People's Republic of China as guests of the Chinese Writers' Association. Much of the credit for orchestrating the trip belongs to Richard Liu of Victoria, who publishes in China and was willing to make all the arrangements with our counterparts in Beijing. The task of getting us there fell to me and required some fancy footwork and prospecting skills; however, thanks to Dr. Fenton Hay of Consumer and Corporate Affairs and some far-seeing individuals in the provincial cultural agencies of Ontario, Manitoba, and Saskatchewan, the 'gang of seven' was eventually air-borne. Once in China, of course, all our needs were taken care of wonderfully by our hosts and we embarked on an experience so moving and instructive that it deserved to be set down for the record.

Chinada is dedicated to the Chinese Writers' Association, to the writers of Canada for whom we were the fortunate first representatives, and to all people of both countries who love literature and the free exchange of ideas.

Gary Geddes

Chinadiary

by Gary Geddes

Departure time approaches. This is no way to begin. I am so tired of the hassles of organizing and fund-raising for this trip, I'd almost rather stay home. Still, there is a groundswell of nervousness that is more than my usual fear of travel by air. Tranquilized butterflies lifting a stained-glass wing at random intervals. Nobody, of course, believes that I'd rather be home with my family and my work. I wonder...

☯

I am reading Hugh Trevor Lloyd's *Hermit of Peking,* about a fascinating scoundrel and uppercrust con named Sir Edward Backhouse. *Un vrai bécosse.* But he had a golden ear for languages. The Chinese have always been astonished to find a Westerner who makes the effort; and I am still struggling with pleasantries and Chinese numbers: "Wo shi Jiànadà yen." I am a Canadian. The simplicity is embarrassing.

☯

What do I leave behind me unfinished? Children, poems, Quadrant, my fledgling publishing venture. And Jan, at a moment of building—lives, barns, fences. The fences are done, good neighbours or not, thanks to my one-eyed friend John Dashney. "If the weather's good tomorrow, I'll go east for a couple of hours." East being my place, a mile down the road. The Great Wall of cedar posts, page wire, and creosote.

☯

Why this constant putting of myself to the test? Last year Quadrant, on the bow-wave of domestic crisis; this year, China. I tell myself that things just happen to me, but it's only half true. I've been laying the foundation for years. Those delicate mushrooms growing out of the wheat-sheaf paper on top of grave-posts in the Chinese graveyard at Cumberland. Currency for the dead. Working with George Liang in Edmonton on translations of Li Po and Tu Fu. My trip to Hong Kong to do research on Canadians interned there during World War II. Then, P.K. Page's introduction to Richard Liu, my Chinese double, teaching Spanish at Shanghai University.

☯

I never wanted to go to Peru after Woodcock, Purdy, Birney, Lane, and Mandel had combed the terrain for poems. Now I find even China has its guest-list of Canadians and other writers. As Galbraith says, "I was struck by how hard it is to be a pioneer anywhere today."

☯

John Meares, what happened after the massacre of the Europeans by Maquinna to the 200 Chinese you brought to Nootka in 1795, to run the tannery there?

10

It's happening. CP Air to Vancouver. Adele, Alice, Geoff, so far so good. Bumped into Eli Mandel at the airport in Toronto, en route to Edmonton. When he heard we were on our way to Peking, he became visibly green. George Johnston is right: "At any given moment in Canada, the sky is black with poets."

☯

Richard Liu at the Vancouver airport advises us about officialdom, protocol. All requests made through Honourable Leader or Responsible Person — me. Suzanne's plane delayed with engine problems, rerouted to Tokyo via L.A. And I have her passport. Kroetsch and Lane are in the bar, as arranged. Bob has a notebook that says ALL TECHNIQUE in bold type on the cover.

"So I finally meet a man who's all technique. You must be a postmodernist."

"No, I'm a romantic. As I get old and lose my technique, I believe more and more in love."

☯

31,000 feet over the Pacific. Backhouse a fraud. Perhaps we all are. Talk of collaborating on a book about China has Patrick writing furiously, me completely dried up. I am going in search of Hoey Shin, a transcendental Buddhist who discovered North America by sea and land fourteen centuries ago. To find the West, he travelled East 30,000 li; I am a high-flying materialist, winging my way West towards a mythical China in a jet plane six miles above the earth.

☯

The buzzer at the Chinese Embassy in Ottawa summons a young man in regulation costume. He ushers me into a waiting-room that contains larger-than-life pictures of Mao, Lenin, and other figures I am less certain of. The successors. Kang Chongru materializes beside me with his interpreter, Mr. Li. We move along the corridor of the former convent on St. Patrick Street into a larger, bare room that contains two rows of not-so-easy chairs with purple leatherette upholstery. No graven images, either Marxist or Christian. Ostentatiously plain, utilitarian, even down to the worker's thermos on the table alongside tea cups with porcelain lids.

What manner of men are these? I cannot tell. Two years away from one's family, in the service of government. A regime more austere and demanding than that of the previous owners. Religion: ideology.

What is that glass case at the far end of the room? I manage a quick peek on the way out — the most exquisite fantasy landscape, or 'scene', constructed of ivory and peacock feathers.

☯

Moonlit Night
Tonight with the moon over Fu Chow
she watches alone inside her chamber.
I pity my children so far hence,
too small to remember Chang An.
The night mist dampens her hair,
renders her arm cold and smooth as jade.
When will we lean together again
in the empty window, moon drying our tears?
                                        Tu Fu

☯

Drunk on saki in Tokyo. I spend the night propped up between the wall and toilet, my head resting on the porcelain bowl. Never mind, the Chinese will reform us. Suzanne has arrived, miraculously.

☯

Touch down unexpectedly in Shanghai. Imagine that, talking to poet Wang Xindi only months after meeting him at the International Poetry Festival in Toronto. A tender welcome. I am ready to be shanghaied.

☯

"...as Madame Ding Ling says so eloquently in her novel, *The Sun Shines Over the Shangkan River,* nobody owns the earth. We also share that belief. We would like to express our gratitude to the Chinese people and to the Chinese Writers' Association for inviting us to share your wonderful homeland. We are deeply moved by your generosity and look forward to being able to reciprocate. As two ancient comrades, Li Po and Tu Fu, came eventually to be linked so often in the public's mind they were referred to as Li Fu, so we will think of you as our friends and will fashion a country of the heart and imagination where we will be co-citizens. We will call that country CHINADA...."

☯

Mr. Bi, liaison officer for the Association, smokes quietly beside me at the poet's lagoon in the New Summer Palace Gardens. Like China itself, he is a survivor; he swims in time, not fighting against it.

"Tell me, Mr. Bi, what would have happened if the Empress Dowager had spent the 10,000 taels of silver on a navy instead of rebuilding these gardens?"

Well fed, comfortable in his own skin, Mr. Bi flicks the ash from his cigarette and replies without hesitation.

"She made the right decision."

❀

Spring Scene
Though empires crumble still the land prevails,
trees and grass reclaim deserted streets.
In times like these the flowers taste my tears,
birdsong troubles my caged and lonely heart.
Three months or more the warning beacon burns,
news from home is worth ten thousand taels.
My white hairs grows so thin with scratching,
a stick of pine will scarcely keep it up.

Tu Fu

❀

Today we are climbing the Wall, literally and figuratively. The Badaling mountains arc around Peking as a natural protection. The Wall adds man's insult to nature's. Stretched out, it would run from Vancouver to Halifax, the longest graveyard in the world. It's too much. Adele is trying to photograph local industry and transport for Dimitri, who was not invited. Alice is looking quiet and self-contained in her harem pants. God knows what she's thinking. At Kroetsch's instigation, we all think of Rudy Wiebe and his novel, *The Blue Mountains of China.* Kroetsch has a postcard for us to sign: "Dear Rudy — Wrong as usual, they're green!"

The plums are also green. Too many consumed. I am the colour of Eli.

❀

14

The Song of Ch'ang-kan

While the hair barely covered my forehead,
I plucked a flower and played at my front door.
You came by riding a bamboo horse
and we circled the well innocent as green plums.
We lived on in the village of Ch'ang-kan,
too young to guess where this might lead.
At fourteen I became your wife,
so shy even my face would not open.
I could not turn once to your insistent call.
At fifteen my eyebrows parted,
I longed to mingle my dust with yours.
I vowed so often to be faithful unto death,
how could I imagine climbing the terrace to watch for you?
At sixteen you went far away
past the Chu Tang Yen Yu rapids:
who dares approach them in the fifth month,
even the ape's cry overhead is sorrowful.
So few people pass my door now
the steps are covered in green moss,
moss so deep I cannot brush it away
and leaves falling in the early autumn wind.
In August the butterflies came,
a pair of them skims the grass in the West garden.
Such things grieve my heart,
my youth is fading as I wait.
Sooner or later you'll come by way of three Pas
and, no matter how far, I will go all the way
to Long Wing Sand to welcome you.

                                                    Li Po

☯

Everyone in a state of shock. Suzanne thinks she's dreaming it all.

◉

Literary Exchange:

Us: Is the preoccupation with realism or naturalism not a red herring?

Them: Writing is not a private enterprise.

Us: How does the writer break new ground using the old literary tools?

Them: I was wrongly labelled as a rightist at 21 and sent off into exile.

Us: Do you believe all literature is propaganda?

Them: I was convinced that the abnormal political life of my party would be rectified.

Us: Realism *is* a red herring.

◉

Lunch with Mary Sun of the Canadian Embassy, then tea with Ding Ling, the most famous writer in China, now free after more than twenty years out of favour. An exercise in contrasts. She reminds me of Margaret Laurence: the price paid shows in the eyes. Exile, confinement, humiliation, forced labour; all those stories lost in the chicken-run.

◉

Thoughts of Li Po From World's End

From world's end the cold wind rises,
how does it go with you my friend?

Will the wild goose come with speed
now that lakes and rivers are swollen?

What things befall the man of words...
dead spirits catch him by the sleeve.

Perhaps you've joined the wronged ghost
of Chin Yuan by now. I'll give this poem

to the deadly waters of Mi Lo.

                                    Li Po

☯

Today I am the hermit of Peking. Or is it Peking Man? Give me a cave to hide away in and brood. Time weighs heavily upon me; yet I feel I must walk tiptoe through China, there's so much history underfoot. Not just the Ming tombs, shrine to a power-monger, a man capable of administering violence and death even from the grave, or the Great Wall reeking of urine. But also a young woman with a string tied to the hind-leg of a squirrel. The leg swollen and bleeding; the squirrel terrified. Little cruelties observed. I have abandoned my camera; speech will be next to go.

☯

Phone call home to Jan. As usual, technology fails us in the moment of intensest need.

☯

Jade Step Complaint

Dew gathers on the jade step,
so late it soaks her silk garments.

Back inside she drops the glass-bead curtain
and watches the translucent autumn moon.

Li Po

☯

Time to leave Beijing. That is the most popular subject in Chinese poetry: departure. I used to wonder why George chose so many poems of departure to translate. Now I know — for him, and for the others.

Li Hanhua plays the harmonica I bought, like an expert. Even Mr. Bi has a go at it, with surprising success. He claims it's the first time in forty years — what prompted that other burst of music all those years past, in the middle of World War II? He gives us a beautiful rendition of Auld Lang Syne. Ah Bi, *toujours le mot juste,* always the right word, the right touch.

"Don't forget us," he says at the top of the escalator, returning my embrace. How could I do that, *péng yoù,* my friend? I descend the moving steps with his personally calligraphed poem in my hands:

He who came to receive gives,
a life more generous than spring.

Where valleys exalt themselves,
the earth freezes.

Only loneliness is plentiful
for the man far from home.

But good friends work together
the way of healing.

Bi Shuowang

☯

Xian. Wang Ronghua and Fan Baoci are still with us. Will we be bodily translated into heaven, after all? Fan does not look old enough to have a son who is an engineer. Wang, a gracious and witty companion, lives with wife, child, and father in one-and-a-half rooms on forty dollars per month. This is his holiday. I remember him in those sunglasses and wearing Patrick's cowboy hat — he looked like a full-blooded Haida. Nothing happened to Meares' two hundred Chinese tanners; they were obviously assimilated.

☯

The garrison army of pottery figures. This is the message I've been waiting for, my notes from underground. I feel the words begin to regroup and march. Then the forest of stele: stonehenge with a written message, poetry on the rocks. My notes are as thin as Tu Fu's hair, but I think the real words will come now — currency for the living. Now I can abandon this infernal diary...

☯

To See A Friend Off

North of the city core the suburbs stretch,
the airport eats its share of real estate.

Here's where we choose to say farewell, amigo,
you with your itchy feet and credit card.

Your mind is lounging in Beirut or Istanbul,
while my heart plummets into gloom.

Wave to me now and be off,
I smell the pollution of your 707.

Li Po, updated *

* All translations but the last were done with the help of George
Liang and will appear in a forthcoming volume called *I Didn't
Notice the Mountain Growing Dark.*

Postcards From China

by Robert Kroetsch

To my daughters,
Margaret and Laura:

July 1

Flying over the Chinese coast, off the China Sea and towards
Shanghai; in the green land far below us, what I took to be
roads. There cannot be so many roads in China, I thought,
roads everywhere. And then, a few minutes later, I realized that
what I took to be roads were canals, ditches, waterways. It was a
web of water below us, the Chinese land.

I thought again of a man I met in the Vancouver Airport,
while waiting for the flight to Tokyo. We were standing in a
check-in line together, this man and I, and when he asked me
where I was going and why I explained that I was going to China
as a writer. And that man, then, was silent for while; and then
he said: I am a man with no language. And he explained: he was
the son of a Japanese soldier stationed in Korea during the Second World War. His mother was Korean. He had not quite
learned Japanese. He had not quite learned Korean. He had

come to Canada and had not quite learned either English or French.

I am in China without a language. What I saw from the sky was roads that weren't roads; I saw the irrigation system for watering the land and from up in the sky I thought I saw roads, too many of them, brown, on the green of the green earth, and then I saw all those roads were water, and so in a sense they were roads, and I thought of the fingering water, holding the land green; it was like that, I has happy to see that, and I understood; but then we were landing.

That was the Shanghai Airport. Now, a few hours later, in Peking, I think of you, my daughters, there on the other side of the world, as innocent of China today as I was yesterday. We come unaware to these tidal changes in our lives.

July 2

You must have a guide when you go on a journey to a mysterious, unknown place; that's one of the rules of literature, and maybe of life also. As it happens, we have three guides, and that makes it even better.

Mr. Bi is one of our guides. Mr. Bi Sho-wang, a stoutish, older man with a face that has seen too much, and therefore he smiles with his eyes instead of with his mouth. He is a poet who knows hundreds of poems in Chinese that he cannot tell us, but he has learned to sing songs in English, and when we are driving around, all of us in a wonderful little bus, seven Canadian writers and our guides and our driver, and when we begin to sing because we are happy, Mr. Bi begins to sing, out of his sad face, songs like "Red River Valley." I suspect he is a direct descendant of a Tang warlord.

Mr. Wang is our translator. He has the tough, wiry body of a rodeo rider, and the tough wiry mind of a poet who is too wise to write poems. He translates with ease and humor and generosity, as if everything said must be wise and good. All the women in our group, Susan Paradis and Alice Munro and Adele Wiseman, are, I can tell, in love with Mr. Wang, who is in love with words and the way they try to buck him off. I know that you would love him too, if you were here.

Our third guide is Madame Fan. Like Mr. Bi she is a poet, and like Mr. Wang she is a translator. She worries about us Canadians. I can see that her assignment is to worry about us. She worries that we aren't eating enough, though we are stuffed with huge meals three times a day, and she worries at the amount of beer we Canadians drink, and she worries that the ferocious sun of this long drought will strike us all down in our tracks and she took us to a small, delightful store and allowed us to buy straw hats. My straw hat is too small. Madame Fan doesn't seem to worry about that, however.

The Forbidden City is a place of magic roofs. The tile roofs are golden and dare to imitate the sun. Only dragons dare to land on the roofs. There are nine thousand rooms in this palace. I have been into ten of them.

Tonight we had dinner with a group of Chinese writers. We had duck for dinner. The whole meal was duck. I've come to like using chopsticks. One member of our party is in danger of starving because she can't use chopsticks. But I like them. Throw away your knives and forks. Eat duck. We started with feet of duck. The gizzard, to me, is not quite so good as chicken gizzard. But the heart is a delicacy. And the head, split open after being roasted, is full of surprises for the palate. Wash all this down with tall brown bottles of Chinese beer. And two kinds of duck soup. Yes, the soup came at the end of the meal. And each and every dish is placed on a lazy susan, in the middle of the round table, and passes before you. And you have to be quick with your chopsticks. Especially to eat soup.

July 3

The bicycle riders are dancing. It is a dance of silence in the long, wide, straight streets of Peking. The wheat is spread to-day, on the pavement, to dry. The dancers are offering praise.

Today we went to many places, and one of them was the New Summer Palace. Yiheyuan. Garden of Harmony in Old Age. I went there hoping to catch a glimpse of Buddha, so I climbed the Hill of Longevity, and damned near died doing it; we all of us climbed up hundreds of stone steps. I saw a lotus, in flower, in a small pond, high up the stairway. A lotus in flower is as beautiful as Peking seen from the Cloud-Dispelling Hall. From halfway up the hill we could see, through a mist of fine rain, down to Kunming Lake and its little boats, down to the golden glazed-tile roofs of Peking, the roofs that are like tent-tops turned ornate and golden, and so beautiful that I knew, secretly, that if I tried I could fly like a dragon and land on a roof. We climbed all the way up the steep stairway to the Pavilion of the Fragrance of Buddha. And we went inside, into the tall, high gloom, into a room that was big enough for Buddha himself. But Buddha wasn't there. But I wasn't surprised, I knew I had climbed the hill to find, to admire, to love a lotus blossom.

We had lunch in the Hall for Listening to Orioles Singing. I was happy, thinking about Buddha, who had stepped out of his Pavilion, somehow, before I got there. I thought about the lotus in blossom and the golden glazed-tile roofs, the tiles like the scales on the most beautiful fish in the world; and we ate fish, and we drank more good Chinese beer. Or maybe I have this wrong. Maybe we ate the lunch and then went and climbed the

24

Hill of Longevity and looked for Buddha. In any case, there was a fine rain falling, more of a mist than a rain, and we could and we couldn't see what we were seeing. And I think it was yesterday we went to the Forbidden City. China is a garden and a maze. We went tonight to the Peking Opera, here, in Peking. And a male actor, a man in his forties, acting in "The Drunken Beauty," in a matter of minutes persuaded me that he was a young woman, and beautiful, and sad, and disappointed in love, and getting drunk. And I am in China.

Imagine my surprise when I sat down beside Joseph Conrad at a crowded table in the rooftop restaurant of the Friendship Hotel. It was a hot night. "It's none of my business, Mr. Conrad," I said, "but, frankly, a lot of people would be surprised to see you here in China." He looked surprised, under his ridiculous white jungle hat. "How so?" he said. "Well," I said. I was being discreet. "You were born in 1857." "Quite so, quite so," he said, trying to sound British. But I could see he had forgotten the year of his birth. He's showing his age. And then he added, suddenly, powerfully, "I've never been here myself." And the voice, Laura; you should have heard him. But I was puzzled by his statement. "I've never been here myself." And there he was, right beside me. I noticed his beer bottle was empty. I jumped up and went into the small room where two young women were sweating in the dim light, one of them snapping the tops off bottles, the other making change for the *yuan* notes, using an abacus. When I got back to the table with the beer, Mr. Conrad was nowhere to be seen. I looked silly, a full bottle in my hand, another at my place. "Thirsty tonight?" someone said. And before I could answer or ask, "It's the drought does it," he said. The stranger. "The worst in two hundred years."

July 4

Tea, in the cool dawn, while I sit at the old and ornate desk, here in my room, and look out under the bamboo strips that shade my window. Hot water from the huge thermos. The tea steeping in a lidded cup.

There are dragons everywhere. Dragons carved in stone.

Painted dragons. Dragons made of tile, of jade. I have asked my guides what dragons stand for and each guide gives me a different explanation. Finally, I begin to understand.

I have come to China to read the future. A Chinese poet can look back to the *Shih-ching,* a collection of poems put together about 600 B.C. Before Plato and Socrates had their confabs.

Today we had lunch in the Canadian Embassy. How quickly knives and forks have come to seem affected, strange, not immediate and direct. Chopsticks, Meggie, become the hand, the fingers. They are becoming.

· Today we had tea with Madame Ding Ling. She works in this newfangled form, the novel. Twenty-one years, she spent, "in the country." For having the courage to speak her truth, a Chinese woman's truth. To go to her apartment is to sit, humbly, in the presence of courage. She has a beautiful granddaughter who reminded me of you; the grand-daughter is studying English... There are dragons, everywhere.

July 5

The Great Wall looks as if it must have kept China in, not the barbarians out. It is a frame on China, a long frame, unimaginably crooked, hung on top of mountain ridges. I walked my feet to blisters, following my eyes.

Two boys selling green apricots, where the buses park, and

we were hungry for fresh fruit and bought apricots from hand-held scales and Gary Geddes and Patrick Lane and Geoff Hancock managed to eat at least enough, perhaps too many.

We had a picnic at the site of the Ming Tombs. A picnic here is not out on the grass, it's out of a basket. We sat around tables in a gracious building that seems to have been prepared, complete with private rooms and waiters, especially for picnics. But the picnic lunch was huge: we ate boiled eggs and great thick slices of bread, and we ate chicken, and we drank the orange drink that seems to be everywhere in China, a version of Orange Crush.

The Great Wall. The Ming Tombs. They are forms of creation that exist independent of literature. So much death in the wall, in the tombs. They are only a few kilometers apart. The wall and the tombs. And everywhere the hard fact of the peasants' lives. People stooped in the rice paddies. Two fishermen on a raft, fishing with cormorants. Four women digging a ditch. The commune houses, low, blending into the earth. The flocks of ducks beside the ponds. The three-horse teams, hauling loads of pipe, of steel rods, into the city. The bicycles, loaded with hay, with crates, with families. The tall willow trees along the road. The fields of eggplant and corn and beans. Wheat spread to dry on a paved highway. The groups of workers, perhaps twenty-five in a group, men and women, young and old, putting fertilizer on the land by hand, the bags of fertilizer spaced about the fields, the workers going with pans to get more fertilizer, then spreading it by hand. In China: hands and hoes and shovels. Feet, in the dust, in the mud.

Peking: the city itself, being rebuilt, and mostly by hand. We took a cab downtown, tonight, and made a mistake in giving directions. We were let off in an area where workers live; we came upon a boy, seated in the narrow street, strumming a guitar. Gary accepted the guitar from the boy and began to play and in a matter of moments we had an audience of two hundred

27

faces, there in the dimly lit street. We sang the surprise of ourselves, we writers, to the astonished audience. To our own ears. Country & Western.

July 6

The National Museum. My ecstasy at seeing the Tang horses. I experienced ecstasy, Meggie. Whatever that is. The Tang Dynasty, 618-907. The horses are singing. What you used to say, Laura, when we rode the carousel, there in the park in Binghamton, New York. Those perfect horses gave me transport. I was, for almost a minute, resident and present and alive in the Tang Dynasty.

Today we flew to Xian. Xian was the capital during the Tang Dynasty. The four-propellor plane. Our keeping cool by fanning ourselves, the folding fans distributed by the stewardess, who is plainly dressed in the Chinese costume, pale shirt and darker slacks and sandals. Blue or green, mostly. The temperature when we landed: 38 degrees Celsius.

Unexpectedly, I saw Buddha. But there were three of him, three statues, surrounded by eighteen disciples, in a hall I entered when I was looking for the place where the great poet, Tu Fu, got drunk and wrote poems. Tu Fu, the Tang poet, was up on top of the Greater Wild Goose Pagoda, having a sip of wine with Joseph Conrad. I could hear them but I couldn't see them. The pagoda was built in 652 to house the Buddhist sutras; Xuan Zhuang walked to India to get them, and then walked back, with 657 sutras, and made the whole trip in a mere 17 years. The pagoda, seven stories high, was built to house the sutras. In the garden around the pagoda I met a young man who has studied English for a few years but had never spoken to a person who speaks English and he spoke to me, he said, "I am studying photography," and when I answered him he was astonished, he couldn't believe that I really understood him, I

28

responded to his comments, but every so often he would ask, "Do you really understand me?" as if I were only being polite, or pretending, and then he realized he was really speaking the language he had studied, and we embraced and had ourselves photographed, because he was studying photography.

July 7

Here, where the Silk Route began. This morning I got up early and had my tea, and then I went for a walk in the bright morning light to watch people doing their exercises, in the parks. And I saw an old man, walking. In a garden. In a garden that to me seemed to be a maze, a pattern of hedges and paths; one of those gardens designed especially to tease us out of our habitual ways. Like the Forbidden City, in Peking, that unfolds and contradicts and confuses with impossible repetitions. He was following paths, the old man, making turns, pleasing himself with surprise and mystery. Himself stopping, now and then; he watched those about him, doing tai chi, while I watched him watching. One could lose the world, here in Xian. There is no music, not a book or magazine, not a neon sign or sound of traffic that is familiar. I was lost and I was trying to find a post office. I wanted to mail you a card I had written. In a Chinese post office there's a little brush and a glue pot, so you can seal your letter.

We visited the Forest of Steles. Housed in what were once Confucian temple buildings. Slabs of stone with, carved on them, pictures and poems. Calligraphy, that art where hand and mind become synonymous. Two young men were making a print, patting a stone with a cloth dipped in ink. The sound of their patting like a muffled drum.

The underground army. Buried in loess by the endless wind from Mongolia. Buried by the emperor, Qin Shi Huang, who united China and built the Great Wall, who buried himself here

29

in his tomb, in 211 B.C. He surrounded his tomb with armies of life-size figures, in *terra cotta,* armed with real weapons. Six thousand figures, horses and men. Peasants, in 1974, digging a well to fight a drought, found ghostly figures in the earth. The archeology of dream. And now, I cannot forget, the handsome men, the proud horses, rising into this scalding heat from the Chinese earth. This breaking into light.

July 8

Up early to fly to Canton. Guangzhou. Fanning ourselves: perhaps the fans fanning are what make us fly. And then we could not get into the airport in Guangzhou, because of a typhoon. We turned and went west, inland again; we found ourselves flying over the karst country of subtropical China; thrust up from the green fields, the towering pinnacles of limestone. It is hardly a mortal landscape, it seems, rather, left over from a dream. The soldiers of that first emperor, back there in Xian, turned into stone. Forever and never, breaking into light.

My last bed, here in China. Over my bed is a huge mosquito net. It hangs from the high ceiling like a cornucopia and covers the whole bed. A banquet, tonight in Guangzhou. With Madame Fan and Mr. Wong. With the gracious poets who host us in this city. Mr. Wang translates our conversation, translates our poems. I read from "Seed Catalogue," here at this feast from a garden world. Lotus seeds. Quails' eggs. Frogs' legs. We drink toasts. Cinnamon wine. A stern-looking waiter fills our delicate glasses, fills them again and again, and again we drink toasts. Seven appetizers and ten main dishes and four desserts. The cat is delicious, Meggie. I am less fond of snake, I don't much like the texture. One could justify a flight to China, simply to eat fresh lichee nuts.

Taking the train, from Guangzhou to Hong Kong. After the typhoon. I sit here, sipping tea from my lidded cup. I watch through the large windows of this modern train. I watch through the windows. The thousands and more thousands of people, out in the ruined fields. The peasants, picking up, after the typhoon. Perhaps a typhoon is a dragon. And now the sky so clear, so calm. The water buffaloes, moving with slow patience, in the rice paddies. The thousands of people, in the fields, in the ditches, on the roads. With shovels and hoes. Threshing rice with little hand-run machines. Men and animals, wading in the water. Men and women and children, together, salvaging the stooked sheaves of rice. Each small sheaf like a paintbrush, raised to the making of this landscape of hope.

China Poems

by Patrick Lane

THE FORBIDDEN CITY

Within the city there is a city that is forbidden.
In it there is a garden with
contorted stones and miniature mountains,
tiny exquisite temples and waterfalls
splashing into pools where ancient fish still swim.
On warm nights when the cherry trees bloom
the old ones dance with their eunuchs and all are beautiful
in their delicate silks and embroidered robes.
Golden fish rise in the ponds like great jewels
and temple bells ring softly in the dew.
Poems are written as the amber wine is poured
and their gaiety is like green jade,
their laughter smooth as ivory,
as they wander among the new palaces and tombs
rising around them like moons in the pale light.

LOTUS

Lotus, delicate as shy laughter,
float in the pond at the ruined palace.
A girl in a thin blue shift, cool in the day,
reads English by the trunk of a willow.
Branches drift in deep water.
There is a chance, if she learns the new
language before the end of summer, she
will be chosen for the university of Beijing.
On the stone bridge, strangers, their faces
white as rare jades, point at the fallen
stones, the worn heads of dragons. They
come from a country that has no past
and they are awed by the wreckage of years.
The bridge they walk upon once carried
the concubine of a prince. She was young
and beautiful in her white silks the one
night he called for her. After that, she
languished in the House of Women.
A lotus, pink as a child's mouth,
opens. The girl by the pond is so still
the strangers on the bridge do not see her
and do not hear as she carefully repeats
their words over and over under her breath.

TOUR BUS

The day is heavy with heat and the fields,
thick with green rice, bend under the sun.
We follow a truck through the red dust
on our way to the Great Wall. A train,
slow and heavy with freight from central China,
labours through a crossing, and the young men
who laughed in the back of the truck
as the wind whipped their smooth black hair
sit talking in their sweat. One of them
finds a cicada among the empty boxes.
He lifts it out and holds it by the wings.

We wait, visitors in our air-conditioned bus,
listening to our guide tell us of the workers
who died constructing the Great Wall.
For every stone in the wall there is a body.
The long train passes into the west.
The lean young man reaches over the edge
and drops the cicada in front of a tire.
They laugh as the truck moves over its body.
The wind begins to whip their hair.
Fields pass, replaced by stunted trees.
Someone in our van points at the far mountains.

HER LAUGHTER

The day is beautiful, and beyond
light catches the ripe fruit of the trees
above the paddies and the patient men
who guide their bullocks through the mud.

Trucks lumber past the melon vendors
and children. The harvest has been good.
All the oracles were correct and the people
smile at the day and the year to come.

A grandfather sits playing with a child.
She laughs as she runs through his hands.
He could catch her but what for? She is
young and her laughter is good in the sun.

THE WORLD TENT

I

And when the city would not fall,
proud Volohai of the Tangut State,
the devious and inventive Khan
sent a message of great cunning
to the leaders of that city
saying he would lead his men home
if he received tribute of
ten thousand swallows.
The joy in the city
was great as the curious tribute
was paid, the people laughing
at the madness of this Khan.
That night the Mongols
tied tufts of cotton wool
on the tails of tribute
and setting them alight
released them. The night came alive
with the flicker of new stars
as the birds returned to their nests.
Beyond the walls the city burst
to fire and while the garrisson
fought the flames, Ghengis
led his men inside the walls
leaving alive in wreckage
only the bright swallows.

II

I hate luxury and exercise moderation
I have only one coat and one food.
I eat the same food and am dressed
in the tatters of my humble herdsmen.
In the space of seven years
I have succeeded in accomplishing
a great work, uniting the whole world
in one empire. I have not myself
distinguished qualities, but as my calling
is high, the obligations incumbent upon me
are also heavy and I fear that in my rule
there may be something wanting.
To cross a river we need boats and rudders.
Likewise we invite sages and choose assistants
to keep the empire in good order.
I implore thee to move thy sainted steps.
Do not think of the extent of the desert.
Commiserate with the people
or have pity upon me
and tell me the means to preserve life.

Found Poem:
Letter from Ghengis Khan in January,
1221, to Ch'ang Ch'un, elderly recluse
and monk living in the Shan-tun
mountains of China, Taoist sage and
seeker of the Philosopher's Stone.

III

The toumans raged and nothing was left
to live in the great city of Chung-hsing
by the orders of the commanders whose orders
were the last words of the warlord, Ghengis Khan:
At the appointed time, annihilate them.

The city was razed, the walls reduced to rubble,
the grasslands burned. The works of art were
smashed and all that was alive was dead.
Then the mourning army bore him home
to the heartland, the high steppes,
the far mountains of his birth,
killing all living things in their path
according to tradition and nothing was spared
as was his will and the will of the people.
He was placed in his war wagon and buried
on the slopes of Burkhan Khaldun
where a solitary tree stood in the sky
and there was placed there eight white yurts,
pavilions for prayer and meditation
and shrines to his memory. His children
who had been trained from birth to war
having been called from the far reaches
stood at his grave
under the canopy of the World-Tent
suspended from the Pole Star's shaft
and listened to the words of the Shaman,
interpreter of Bai Ulgan, god of the upper air
and, under Tengris, the one true power,
as he read the legacy:

Believe nobody, never trust an enemy,
obey my laws, my Yasak, and carry
every action you begin to its conclusion.

IV

The beautiful, the daughter
of Ghengis Khan watched
unmoved upon her small horse
as every living creature
down to the infants,
down to the very rats,
was butchered and then
beheaded, the heads
flung on a growing pile
which, rotting under
the falling Persian sun,
stood at last a giant tower
of one hundred thousand
skulls. The beautiful,
the daughter of the Khan
who was the Punishment of
God, rode away satisfied
back three thousand miles
of desert, steppe and mountain
having avenged her husband
who was slain
here at white Nishapur
beneath the fallen walls.

V

One can conquer an empire on horseback,
But one cannot govern it from there.

> Memorial presented to Kublai Khan by
> his Confucian adviser in 1261.

But on the high steppes there were those
who remembered the days and nights of Ghengis,
the long marches and the fallen cities.
They thought of the error at Karakorum;
these ones who waited beneath the World Tent,
who still rode the small hard horses
and slept in the yurts of their ancestors.
They came as warriors to Kublai, the Wise Khan,
and bowed before the family right of blood
but they noticed his fingernails, long
and unsuited for war, his Chinese women,
soft and delicate, langorous as willow
leaves on the water of a sleeping lake.

They listened in silence to the advisers
who were Confucians and who believed
that humanity and magnanimity could rule
men, and they bowed low before the throne
and rode out through the rising walls of Ta-tu
back to the tundra and the green taiga
and waited by their fires for the dynasty
to end. They knew no empire can live
that is only governed; only the empire
that conquers again and again can truly
be said to live, for humanity and magnanimity
are as paper money in a burning city, ash
swirling like words in the clear bright flames.

VI

THE GREAT WALL

There is a moment on the wall when a man looks out
over the far horizon and wonders when
when they will come. He does not know who they are.
The wall was built many years ago, long
before he was born and before his father was
born. All his life has been spent
repairing the wall, replacing the fallen
stones, clearing away the tough grass
that grows like fingers in the masonry.

Inside the wall the land is the same
as outside and once, when he was confused
by the hot wind, he could not remember
which side of the wall he lived on and he
has never forgotten the doubt of that day.
He has seen no one but his family for years.
They were given this work by someone
a long time ago or so his father said
but who it was he did not remember,
it was before his time.

But there comes a moment, there always does,
when a man stops his work, lays down his tools,
looks out over the dry brown distance
and wonders when they will come, the ones
the wall is meant for. At that moment
he sees between the earth and the sky
a cloud of dust like the drifting spores
of a puffball exploded by a foot.

He knows there is nothing to do but wait,
nothing he can do but stand on the wall. Everything
is in order, the wall as perfect as a man
can make it. It does not occur to him
that the cloud might be only a cloud of dust,
something the wind has raised out of nothing
and which will return to nothing. For a moment
he wonders what will happen when they come.
Will they honour him for his work, the hours
and years he has spent? But which side
of the wall do they come from?
No one has ever told him what would happen.

He will have to tell his son, he thinks,
his wife. He wishes his father were alive
to see them coming, but he is not,
and his son, who has already learned
the secrets of stone, is asleep.
It is a day to remember.
In all his life he has never been more
afraid, he has never been happier.

SILK FACTORY

The factory is warm and the lines of machines
clatter as shuttles carry thread
through the weave of dragon and phoenix.
White brocade falls from the looms
and the red silk and the white. A weaver-girl
laughs at a young man and he trips on nothing.
When she moves he cannot see where he is going.
Grey with silk dust, windows rattle
and the glass is frosted with snow.
The bitterness of Ch'en T'ao is long ago
and the shuttles are no longer lumps of ice.
Still, the brocade the weaver-girl makes
is not for her, and the young man, though
he labours for many years, will never buy
the white silk she works so hard to weave.

COMMUNE GIRL

It is evening and the geese are lost in their feathers.
Crane flies flutter in the glow of the lamp. Tired,
the woman weaves paper thread through the last firecrackers.
There are almost enough. Market day in Huang-chou.

In a voice dry as chaff from winnowed rice
she sings 'The Girl by Green River' quietly
so her husband and sons, tired from driving
the bullocks through the new fields, do not waken.

A young voice joins her from the corner of the room.
Her daughter, because of the moon
and the warm night, is restless and cannot sleep.
Already she is thinking of a man.

THE DREAM OF THE RED CHAMBER

I cannot find the symbol of the crane on the silver
ink-boxes. Tarnished with dust they lie among
the scarred jade bats and scattered lions.
On the walls hang dresses from the Ch'ing.
Their stitching reveals the faded
dance of chrysanthemums. I search for the ancient
in the clutter of dynasties. An old woman
walks with slowness among the curios.
Her feet are bound. They are the last illusion
in a world that no longer believes such pain is
beautiful. What I want to take back from China
is found only in my dream of the red chamber.
Ashamed, I walk into the crowds on the street
where young women, bright as birds,
run laughing among the Wu t'ung trees.

MOUNTAIN

High on a mountain above a palace
sits a temple, small in the sun. There
Chiang Kai-shek was captured. It was night
and the Red Army surprised him as he slept.
He leapt from a window, trying to escape,
and ran the narrow path to the mountain,
alone and nowhere to go.

At times all history comes down to this:
a small man, running in his pajamas,
desperate, fearing he will die
or, worse, be chained as a vassal
to an empire far to the west and live
his last days on an island in the sun.

OVER THE SLOW RIVERS

Sing swallows, small warriors in the empires
of the branches. The trees will not tire of you
and the bridges over the slow rivers
will shelter your nests as the winds
carry you in the bright battles of air.

Sing to me of the tireless, the endless,
the coming and the going that are leaves:
sing the female and the male of things
among the empires of the air, bright warriors,
none as swift as you in the blue worlds.

CONVERSATION WITH A GUANGZHOU POET

I fought the Japanese here and here
they killed my mother and my youngest son.
There in the mountains, where the green
meets that line of clouds, we fought
their army with rifles
we won from the dead.

The Japanese were quartered on this street.
They controlled the towns and thought
they'd won the war, but we controlled
the real China from the jungle
and in the bamboo groves and hills
where we sat around the small fires
making poems
and cleaning our new rifles.

AGAINST BLUE JADE CURTAINS

For the companions

Against blue jade curtains
friends talk with first friends,
sadness and the touch of wine.
Our loss is our beginning.
Outside bats dance.
They pay us little attention.
Such knowledge is a blessing.
With wine we too hang upside down,
our laughter the flight of bats,
a small but perfect freedom.

FOR ADELE AND DING LING

Our train winds beside the Pearl River and the hills.
My new friend tells of the time when she was young
and waited at the border, wanting to enter China,
to see Ding Ling. Thirty years have passed since then.

Her strong hands hold the bag containing her mother's
dolls, the one thing she brought to show the Chinese.
Of all our gifts, hers was best.

Even the men, so polite and reserved, laughed as she told
the stories of her mother's art. *For the children,*
she would say. The women circled her like flowers,
and Ding Ling. She is quiet as we near the border.

China is already far away. If it is true that for each
gift you leave behind, you carry something away,
then, of all of us, she is the richest.

Through the Jade Curtain

by Alice Munro

When I went to China, I had a colour in my mind. I expected the country to be brown, a beigey, dusty sort of brown, the landcape to be barren, and buildings to be mud-brick but a very sandy colour. Of course, I'd seen pictures of the major things, so I expected them to be there.

Actually, I had a kind of terror about going. I'm often pleased to travel, excited to be going anywhere — I'll even go to Buffalo on a trip. But I was not enthusiastic about going to China at first. It's the sort of thing you don't turn down, but I felt overwhelmed at the idea, that nothing would be familiar enough to touch me at any point.

☯

It was the people, the thing I came back with most of all. It kept occuring to me that there probably were lots of people there who'd never been alone in a room in their lives. There is no *alone* in China. You know, the way the streets are just full of people, day and night; there was just this moving river of people in and out of the buildings, on the streets. I'd never, never had that feeling of crowds, especially crowded fields where so many people were working. The first week when I was back in Ontario and would look into a field and see one enormous machine instead of a hundred people, it seemed very strange; and the streets seemed terribly empty.

☯

The Chinese wanted to get us from one big place to another, but all I wanted was the in-between bits. I wanted to look into courtyards. I had the impression of *indoors*, and crowdedness in small places, but I saw far too little. I don't remember windows very much. Because I live in the country, that's what I wanted to see; I wanted to see what farm life was really like.

I went home early, so I missed the communal farm. But I remember some interesting use of the land, corn growing in apple orchards, or maybe they were peach orchards. Anyway, corn was growing under and between the trees, which we don't do. I thought corn needed more sunlight than that; obviously it doesn't.

I remember the terraced slopes and the mirrors set up along the twisting roads up to the Great Wall, like giant hand-mirrors, lady's hand-mirrors, set up at the curves. It looked so strange.

☯

You could look around while the officials were making their set speeches and see what people had on the walls, all sorts of things. And that was the most fun. I also looked a lot at the way people were dressed. There was a girl with me while we went through the museum. I said: "That's a pretty dress." She got very excited, because it was a pretty dress but by our standards a fairly simple one. She began to tell me how she had to search for material, and a pattern, to make that dress, because it was impossible to buy a dress that had so much style. So we began to talk about clothes; and it was great. She said, "You know, you can't buy clothes for anyone who is..."; then she said "tall", but I knew she meant anyone who had a good figure. She couldn't say anything so vain, but she shaped a waist with her hands. She was lovely.

Then, of course, there was Mr. Wang, who was so marvelous. I often think of him and wonder how he's doing. You felt such a sense of humour there, and of irony, and several levels of thinking about things. It was comforting for me to know that such humour existed, and had survived, in China.

☯

You know, I remember details of the places we stayed in more than I do the postcard scenes of sites we visited. And of the feelings I had in places. I remember an awful feeling in the Ming tombs; I got quite uneasy. There was a sense of horror in that place. I remember the great climb to find the Buddha who wasn't there, but, mostly, I remember the armchairs, the red armchairs in the fancy room where Adele gave the party. And the curtains on my bedroom window, and all those details very clearly, the details of ordinary domestic life as I could see it — though, of course, this was supposed to be a fancy hotel room. Other things tend to be a little more remote. I can see them, and describe them, but they don't come back too well. They have a sense of arranged beauty, which is always admirable; but my own response to it fades rather quickly and I want to just look at ordinary things, which stay with me.

☯

The writers were a little more careful than I expected — and I had expected them to be careful. As I remember it, there was

53

not much communication there at all. They talked about writing in the service of the State pretty much; and how well the State cared for its loyal servants. Quite possibly they'd been chosen precisely because they'd shown no signs of being interested in writing the way we do. But I was a little disappointed — no, very disappointed — at the time, because I hadn't expected quite so firm a party line. I had thought things were opening up enough so we could talk of literature in other ways. It reminded me a lot of the way people talked in Huron County, when we were having the dirty books fuss there and some people got up and said dirty books were alright because they showed you how terrible life was and they taught you a lesson, but everybody had in mind that literature is there to teach lessons. So I thought they were very like the Methodists of my childhood. At least that was the *sound* of things; I don't know what their writing is really like, whether there are ways to get around all that, to get things said.

Still, they were all so charming, so pleasant. I can imagine that censorship in such a context would be more a matter of gentle persuasion. Most people would be convinced, more or less naturally, that writing was for certain purposes. I could see that it might be something they would buy fairly easily, because I grew up in this Methodist environment where there were very definite ideas about literature. They weren't being enforced, but they were there. I can still get that feeling when people say, "Is it necessary to have all this sex in books?" And I know exactly how a censorship can be enforced without anybody ever having to be rapped on the knuckles.

☯

A couple of women came up to me after my talk about women in literature and started telling me of how their husbands wouldn't help with the housework. And we got into a very vehement conversation about this, how difficult it was. Most of them thought that the system would eventually eradicate all such reactionary ideas and behaviour. In China, there must be the practical difficulty for women of having to do too much work, but then in other ways it probably is much easier, to cover your ways, not to have big families and never be expected to — though maybe that's a great sorrow to women who want more children.

I don't think the lives of women in China differ very much anymore from the lives of men. Everybody has their advantages and disadvantages.

☯

A fiftieth birthday in China? I thought it was gorgeous; I thought it was just marvelous! Because a fiftieth birthday is something that you're a little scared of. Fifty, to me, always sounds a little grey — something kind of withered about it. And there I was having this wonderful banquet in Guangzhou. And then my birthday went on in Hong Kong and across the Pacific and finally it sort of petered out as we approached Vancouver. I think it was still my birthday when we got in to Canada — it was, it went on for days. And it was a wonderful way to be fifty. It was the greatest birthday of my life.*

From an interview with Geoff Hancock.

China Album

Getting there. Top: Narita Airport, Tokyo. Bottom: Beijing.

Talking with Mary Sun, Cultural Attaché at the Canadian Embassy.

First round of talks. Top: Fan Baoci (second from left) and Wang Ronghua (right), with interpreters studying English. Bottom: members of The Chinese Writers' Association in Beijing, including Li Jiang, Tsou Difan, and Guo Lou.

Top: the gang at the Friendship Hotel, Beijing. Bottom: with Mr. Bi at the Poet's Lagoon in the New Summer Palace Gardens.

Geoff at the Temple of Heaven.

Top: Bob, Alice, and Patrick. Bottom: Patrick, armed with guidebook, making small talk with mythological beast.

The studhorse men, or how to be transported in China.

Construction and deconstruction in Beijing.

Alice, stepping out.

Bi Shuowang, liaison officer for the Association in Beijing.

Ruins of the Old Summer Palace Gardens, sacked by the Foreign Devils.

Adele and Geoff.

Top: Ding Ling in her apartment with her grand-daughter and Alice Munro. Bottom: Ding Ling and Li Jiang.

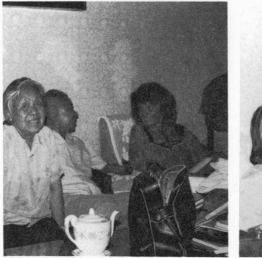

Gary with one of Adele's 'friends'.

Suzanne, pensive.

Patrick and Alice hamming it up in the Badaling Mountains near Beijing.

Adele, climbing the Wall.

Gary and Patrick, on sentry duty: waiting for the Barbarians.

Left: Patrick with Wang Ronghua. Right: Bob with stone beast along the Way of the Spirit near the Ming Tombs.

Bob and Alice, taking a breather.

Gary, on top of the details at last.

The gang with Fan Baoci.

Top: At the Whispering Wall. Bottom: At the Forbidden City with Mr. Bi, Wang Ronghua, and Li Hanhua.

Geoff with Chinese spirits.

Our guides in front of National Museum, with poster celebrating the anniversary of the Congress of the Chinese Communist Party.

Alice and Patrick.

Official portrait of the gang in Beijing.

Mr. Wang with Adele's dolls.

In Xian with members of local branch of the Association, including Yang Weixin, Mao Qi, and Li Xiaoba.

Patrick in formal attire.

Two literary enthusiasts in Xian, debating the function of art.

Casting a disapproving eye on the antics of the gang of seven.

Top: Unexpected stop in Guilin, thanks to #6 typhoon. Bottom: nursery children on a walk in Guangzhou.

Bob and Wang Ronghua in Guangzhou.

Top: Wei Qui (right) and our friendly driver at Heavenly Lake lookout. Bottom: Wang and Fan with friends from Guangzhou branch of the Association: Wei Qui, Quang Qing Yun, Yu Ru, and staff member.

Back
Home

Richard Liu with Ding Ling and Chen Ming in front of Bethune's birthplace in Gravenhurst, Ontario.

Top: Ding Ling and Chen Ming at Niagara Falls. Bottom: Ding Ling talks with Chinese students at York University in Toronto.

Ding Ling at Maison du Thé restaurant in Montreal.

How To Go To China:

by Adele Wiseman

What actually happens turns out to have been, perforce, inevitable. Even if it is manifestly impossible at the time and you can't believe it and afterwards you know you must have been dreaming, it has the authority of having actually happened.

☯

What we dream, what we want, what we conceive as possible, what we attempt but fail to achieve, what engages us, where we direct our hearts and our minds, all these have their own authority too, and in the course of a lifetime may be seen to have weakened and perhaps even, in places, broken the barriers between the impossible, the possible and the actual.

☯

What is so interesting is the interchangeability of the emotions and responses we assume to be appropriate to the actual and to the imaginary. Thus my first childhood visits to China and my abortive trip around the world in search of The People's Republic feel as real as, and ultimately are a part of, my actual visit, while the actual visit has from the first appeared to me to be as unreal as a gloriously self-fulfilling dream which still continues.

☯

1932-5   FIRST COMINGS AND GOINGS

I dug a hole to China in the sandbox. I went down through the melted middle earth in a heat-proof elevator I invented. People down there hung from the bottom of the world by their feet head first into the sky under them. I popped out among them standing on my head and waving my feet. I thought they were upside down. They thought I was wrongside up. They turned me over and showed me they were all right for their side of the world. They showed me a lot of things and then I got in my elevator and came home. I popped out in my own backyard standing on my head and waving my feet. I said "Don't just stand there. Turn me over."

Another way to go to China is to go straight up. When you get far enough up you stop and just wait in a piece of sky. When the earth has turned so China is under you you drop down again. This time you arrive right side up.

So if you want to go to China either you or the world have to turn over.

☯

SUMMER 1960   TRIAL RUN AROUND THE WORLD

The monk Hsuan Tsang who went from China to India to

bring back the Buddhist scriptures took along the wilfull, pugnacious, inventive Monkey King as his assistant. Through circumstances about which I have written elsewhere, *(Old Woman at Play),* that monkey has been my totem from prenatal times. The signs of Monkey King's influence are not so much visible as tonal. It is the quality of your life's adventures which reveal you to be under his particular protection.

I had participated in the Sino-Japanese war by passionately boycotting Japanese pencils. My head was abuzz with histories of Chinese civilization, accounts of The Long March; my conscience was troubled by grim stories of Western depredations in China. Reports of what was going on now in The People's Republic didn't seem to make much sense, so a friend and I decided to go in there and do a picture book. Her camera and my words would capture the real truth and initiate a new era of understanding and cooperation between East and West. The project was ideally suited to the temperament of a penniless young writer who was more worried about being trapped into having to look for a job appropriate to her insignificance than about what might happen if by any chance she did find herself wandering in post-revolutionary China with a few words of self-taught Mandarin (set to her own music) and forty ideograms imperfectly stowed in the aerie pockets of her head.

Out of the eight hundred fifty odd million inhabitants of The People's Republic of China at the time, I fully expected to meet one particular woman, the revolutionary writer Ting Ling. Her name delighted me, full of bells and music and good feelings. She had to be special. I imagined some slender, exotic loveliness, I suppose a wood or water creature, oriental variety, dryad of naiad, but with guts. She was clearly the centre of a somehow portable salon in which the basic principles and the moral and aesthetic aims of the revolution were constantly being improved and expressed while the revolution pressed on to the ultimate perfection to which the revolutionary writer's work gave always the true compass direction. Had I heard then of a cultural revolution in the offing, I would have assumed that if it

100

was worthwhile my future friend Ting Ling must be somehow in the van.

The full story of that journey around the world in search of China will have to await another telling. Suffice to say it actually happened. I scrounged a few bucks. My friend conned a free trip on a Greek coal-carrying cargo freighter heading from Norfolk, Virginia, through the Panama Canal across the Pacific to the Southern Straits of Japan. At the last minute she decided to fly. We arranged a rendezvous at the Dai-ichi Ginza Hotel in Tokyo and I was off, to my astonishment, alone.

Something over a month later, I found that my friend had checked out of the Dai-Ichi Ginza and had established herself comfortably in Wright's Old Imperial. She had also got herself engaged to a distinguished American scientist she'd met over the smörgasbord table. It was fated that I should sink my coal grimy ankles in those lush carpets and flop in that elaborate Japanese-American gingerbread luxury that was built to withstand earthquakes but not, apparently, 'progress,' because not too long afterwards it disappeared forever.

We threaded our way between the mist-girdled little green island jewels of the Japan Inland Sea to Hong Kong on a British freighter which failed to get permission to pick up cargo in Shanghai. On the mainland we managed to get as far as the border bridge at Lo Wun. We stood yearning towards the hills dotted with the graves of Overseas Chinese, many of them Canadian, who had saved enough to make the final trip home, but hadn't been able to get beyond the scrim of border hills either. I was disappointed that politics had plugged up the sandboxes, but could not really blame the Chinese for deciding that they did not need me. Not for the last time was I to confront the patent fact of my irrelevance with the modestly comforting thought of having got so far in spite of it. I did not, of course, know at the time that Ting Ling had already entered her severe and lengthy period of chastisement.

I did not lose hope entirely. As I set off for London and the wedding of my friend, a certain simian, whose religious name is

Wu K'ung (He Who Understands Vacuity), was slyly declaiming within, "I shall return." An excerpt from my diary reads: "Perhaps some day if we really set our hearts to it it will be as easy as dreams to go to China."

Oddly enough, many years later, it was.

☯

SUMMER 1981   HOW TO GO TO CHINA FOR REAL

1. **Get invited**
2. **Along with six other Canadian poets, fiction writers and editors**
3. **Do everything Gary Geddes, your leader, tells you to do, but don't say "Yes Monkey King, No Monkey King" out loud.**
4. **Never, for a moment, actually believe it's happening or is going to happen. This time, no ideograms, no mock scholarship. Just don't get in the way as one by the obstacles are swept away by the disembodied voice of your leader over the telephone, and by the invisible magician Richard Liu.**
5. **At the same time as you refuse to be so unsophisticated as to believe, know absolutely, deep inside you, beyond belief or disbelief, that every little gesture of every little spade from the very first instant many years ago has in fact been moving you inevitably Chinaward.**

It was like doing a re-run of an earlier part of my life, only this time getting it right. And this time it was happening with frills on. I had never, for instance, travelled with a bunch of literary notables before. I could imagine the seven of us watching each other, could feel myself becoming six different works of fiction, more, when I thought of the many Chinese writers we

would be meeting who would be bouncing us off their imagina-
tions as we were bouncing them and each other. The atmosphere
of high idiosyncratic consciousness was going to be, to say the
least, invigorating. I had to warn myself not to get so interested
in writer-watching I'd miss China after all. But what a bonanza!

☯

FROM MY NOTES:

Young Geoff Hancock immediately reveals himself the
quintessential traveller. When we pile into an empty carriage in
the train that is to take us into Tokyo from the Narita airport it
is Geoffrey who bothers to check the tickets to find we have
sprawled out in the wrong carriage. Alice Munro chats quietly,
exchanging maternal queries with me about things that really
count, but her eyes and her occasional sudden comments reveal
she never misses a nuance of interaction going on about her.
Robert Kroetsch is massively serious, attentive. He sits beside
the white gloved Japanese taxi driver as we race through the
darkened streets and under overhead spaghettiways, reminiscent
of the old el of New York City. We pass sudden splashes of
gaudy light from occasional bazaars. The taxi driver up front is
explaining to Bob, in Japanese, with mounting desperation,
what will turn out to be the fact that all the hotels in the Ginza
are Ginza hotels, and he can't take us to the Ginza hotel till he
knows which Ginza hotel we want. Robert soothes him with
sounds that grow ever more expressively musical, com-
municating a largeness of goodwill that must inevitably lead to
mutual understanding on some higher level than the merely ver-
bal. We are taken to the wrong hotel. Our leader, Gary, sets patiently to work and establishes finally that our hotel is the Dai-
ichi Ginza. Of course. And me only twenty one years late for my
reservation.

We are still tourists during that short day we spend together in Japan. Alice and I rush off to find a department store to buy some rope to tie up the big suitcase I'd brought full of Canadian books for our hosts of the Chinese Writers' Association. It had burst open from sheer literary weight. We eat a feast of raw seafood and beer in a sushi bar and gradually accept the magic of being here this way, a magic which will never quite leave us. Patrick Lane, for instance, in the head-turning leather cowboy hat, spends a long time assigning most of us new names for our journey. Pat becomes Turtle with No Head, Geoff Hancock, Serpent with One Fang, Alice Munro is Flying Crane, Bob Kroetsch is White Pine Tree, and I, One Wing Stone, am reminded that Monkey was said to have been born from a stone egg, and was called Stone Monkey.

We spend hours wandering around the Emperor's palace walls and gardens. I finally prove to myself as well as the others that the huge, gorgeously colored Emperor's carp I remember from last time do exist in the moat and come up to be fed just like public ducks do elsewhere. I am amused and delighted at the passion my male companions have for facts. They all know so much, read up on everything, are so generous in exchanging their information. I am older than all of them but an incurable kid sister where information gathering is concerned, and am perfectly content to learn by listening. I was right not to swot up in advance.

☯

JULY 1, 1981

The Air China flight sets down first, briefly, in Shanghai, where our little British freighter hadn't been able to stop twenty one years ago. The temperature is a clammy 86° but the cold beer is very passable. At the airport in Beijing (Peking) we are greeted by a deputation of our hosts from the Chinese Writers'

Association, and by our Cultural Attache Dr. Mary Sun come straight from a Canadian Embassy party celebrating CANADA DAY. How the divine powers beyond comprehension have orchestrated our arrival. We feel it, every one of us. In Beijing, The Golden City, we cease to be merely tourists. However haphazard a group of literaries we may have begun by being, in Beijing the mantle descends on the motley. Certainly, our quiet, attentive Quebecoise member, Suzanne Paradis makes it clear we come from a country that does not lack for dissent. But we have become, however unofficial, ambassadors, determined to represent our country and professions honestly, and at our best, and equally determined to make this cultural exchange as real a dialogue as possible.

Not that my resident spirit monkey is likely to allow this sense of responsibility to weigh too heavily. He knows me from the inside out, a triumphant child wearing a fat, middle aged woman, wearing a blue straw fedora, who is thrilled to her square, bare toes to have her sandals at last planted solidly on Chinese soil. The child within the self-styled ambassador is mad with joy; the middle aged woman is unable to wipe the fatuous beam from her face. She has just heard that tomorrow night the Vice-Chairman of the Chinese Writers' Assocation is going to host the first feast in our honour. The Vice-Chairman is the famous revolutionary feminist writer who was only released a couple of years ago from her lengthy punitive ordeal. Her name, in the new reformed spelling, is Ding Ling.

Night falls early in July on the other side of the world. The air conditioned little mini bus, prototype of all the little buses in which we are to make our many journeys during the next eleven days, takes us, honking almost continuously through the broad main thoroughfares of Beijing, to the Friendship Hotel compound. For long stretches we are the only motorized vehicle around. Groups of people sit in circles on the road under the streetlamps, playing cards. We weave clamorously over meridians, around tooling bikes, squatters and strolling pedestrians. We pass a huge billboard which describes graphically and optimistically the basic principles of controlled traffic flow. People squat on the sidewalks, play games on the dusty earth, stand reading under the streetlamps. It is strange and exotic and yet it is somehow familiar. What does it feel like?

Childhood. There is something about the pace of the evening, the people sitting around, even the darkness and the human clusters under the sparse lights, the streets almost empty of motors but still alive with people. There is a whole different feeling to a world which is closer than ours to the natural pattern of dark and light, a world where people don simple, loose clothes and sit on the ground in the hot summer evenings, chatting, playing games, holding books up to the weak artificial light, letting themselves modulate into the night. On hot, clammy summer nights in Winnipeg, after my hard day's work of digging we used to go out and lie in the yard, or on the boulevard. The earth wasn't dirt in those days.

During the day vehicles crowd these streets, many bicycles, often rigged up to carry enormous loads, mechanical mules pulling every conceivable sort of vehicular contraption, horses, donkeys, mules, sometimes incongruously coupled, or in threes, with one to the side of the load, and those carts with the two large wheels which are so neatly balanced that the human between the shafts often guides rather than pulls them along the flat streets. Nothing is waste here. Long, flat wagons with oval tanks on them carry 'nightsoil' (what our soldiers in Italy and France used to call 'honey wagons' during the Second World War), to be treated and used for fertilizer. Even the metal scrap leavings after stamping are used as fences. The city is remarkably tidy, though a lot of building is going on. It is considered, I'm told, 'the most unfinished city.'

The pattern of our visit is established in Beijing. We are to be the guests of the Writers' Association branches in three major cities, Beijing, XiAn the ancient inland capital of many dynasties of emperors, and Guangzhou, (Canton). During most

106

of the day we will be taken sightseeing to points of interest within and in the environs of our host cities. Late afternoons and evenings we meet with our hosts, explain ourselves to each other, read to each other, feast and talk shop. In Beijing, Suzanne has a special French-speaking interpreter assigned to her. Mr. Bi Shuowang, Head of the English Translation Service of the Writers' Associaton, is in constant attention to our comfort, and a whole variety of interpreters and translators place themselves at our service during our trips. At one point we count five for the seven of us. Travelling with us, giving the entire journey a grateful continuity and consistency, and adding to the experience the gifts of their unfailing patience and warmth, are our two superb guides, interpreters and good companions, Fan Pa-Otze (Baoci) and Wange Wang Ronghua.

☯

BRIEF PAUSE:

Writing this a year after the experience, I find my memory of events is kaleidoscopic. Every time I shake my head different pieces fall together in an extraordinarily rich series of impressions, gifts, lessons, patterns, revelations, fulfillments, and, no growth without some pain, the odd 'ouch.'

☯

FROM MY NOTES:

Swallows swooping under the wingy eaves of the Temple of Heaven, with its brilliant blue tiled roof and gold knob of the sun. In my mind a blur of beauty. The city earth and stone is grey with a bluish cast to it, a tranquillizing effect, which combines and contrasts marvelously with the lavish and varied colouration of palaces, temples, pagodas. The vivid roofs shimmer, masses of cobalt blue tile, gleaming green, burning gold in the sun. Intricately carved fences and ornaments and bas reliefs of glittering white stone and delicate bronze figures; brilliant, dramatic crimsons and the most subtle of shadings (those rich, oxblood walls!) Chinese tourists too wander about, soldiers, peasants, occasionally an old woman with the pony feet in tiny slippers of a thankfully begone age, and whole families, the young children with slitted pants for easy and sensible evacuation. They too appear a little stunned, perhaps trying to assimilate the fact that countless generations have paid and earned for them this heritage.

We cannot avoid learning something of our own heritage either, here, though so far away from home. In the old Forbidden City, there are marvelous huge gold lions with pups and pearls, and great gilded metal vessels. Some of the hugest pots have had the gilt completely scraped off. This was done, we are told, by order of one of the generals of the eight invading armies. He later became a Governor General of Canada, "if it doesn't offend you," says my informant, and the scrapings presumably went with him.

I have to wince again on the site of the ruins of the Old Summer Palace, sacked and burned in a gratuitous object lesson of the invading armies of the West, lest the Chinese be tempted to resist occupation. Wandering about among the sins of the Western fathers, here, we startle the occasional brown chicken and encounter some shy young people from the neighbouring commune cultivating herbs. I hear Suzanne behind me murmuring "domage," and Bob says something about "the poetry of destruction." It is a curiously peaceful scene, with us scrambling among those tall, perilously balanced broken pillars and pediments, whose ornamentation too implies a definite Western influence, and hearing from over the distant ponds and across the fields, Chinese voices singing in chorus from the commune. The small gifts of polished, broken shards of tile which we are given, from the rubble, constitute a complex remembrance. Thank goodness our hosts keep reminding us that Norman Bethune was also a Canadian.

ATTITUDES TOWARD US?

A great deal of curiosity, sideways glancing and circling around us, attempts not to stare overtly as well as frankly overt staring. Reactions sometimes of fright from little kids, and several times I suspect (and am confirmed by the others) deliberately orchestrated jostlings which sabotage some of my camera clicking, or sudden appearances, timed with admirably mischievous skill, which cut off my view.

On the whole, the general mannerliness of people far outweighs the occasional irritability. And when the essential warmth and humanity and gaiety of the Chinese bubble up to greet us, as they do so often, from beaming strangers in the street, what a pleasure! Nobody smiles so irresistibly.

VIGNETTE:

I'd been warned that just about everything worth seeing in China has to be climbed. Wang Ronghua encourages me up the HILL OF LONGEVITY with stories of how often his elderly parents have made it up these steep steps to where the most famous Buddha is enshrined. I pantingly assure him that I think I've probably seen a picture of this Buddha. Is he an all-gold one? Is he sitting? A big stone one with palm out, fingers up? Mr. Wang replies that I will find the Lake of Wisdom at the top of the hill. Labouring, I gasp, "Is it a natural or man-made lake?" I begin to recognise that if I survive this climb I will already have achieved an unexpected longevity. When we actually make it there is no visible lake, and the plain doors are barred; no Buddha to be seen with the eye. I descend, older and wiser, and oddly pleased to have been so nicely teased by my literal-mindedness up into the vital life of a metaphor.

OLDEN DAYS GOLDEN DAYS

A mind boggling visit to the State Museum in Tien Amen Square. I will not begin to speak of the pottery and porcelain or I will not be able to stop. It is interesting to hear from one of the young women interpreters accompanying us that she and her friends voluntarily helped with the building of the museum, which was only completed last year. It's an austere but graciously proportioned place with a golden roof and coloured decorative strip just below the roof, matching those of the buildings across the huge square. That square, which is decorated with huge banners on which are painted oddly pretty portraits of early communist leaders and theoreticians of both China and Russia, can pack a million people.

In the museum, Alice and I admire an intricately filigreed ancient iron artifact, tube shaped, with a little door in it and a curious little handle that puzzles me slightly. She thinks what a nice mantel ornament it would make, until we are told, "That's to chop off a person's left leg!" Sure enough the puzzling knob resolves itself into a man with a short left leg holding a kind of crutch.

Historical material here is interwoven with modern paintings done in the old style, of early famous uprisings in Chinese history, now seen as precursors to the one which produced today's China. We all seem to do a variant of this, a selective

110

realignment of the past to project inevitability onto a hopefully postulated future. But what a past there is here to select from!

❀

DING LING:

I have been hesitating about what for me personally was the journey's most generous gift, because I know I cannot tell it well enough. So I will simply set it down.

The evening of the Peking Duck banquet was our first introduction to some of the illustrious members of the Chinese Writers' Association. Gary suggested we bring along the books which we wanted to leave with the National Office (Beijing branch). That meant roughly a third of what I had brought. I found they were so heavy I couldn't trust them to plastic bags. So I put them in one of the big, sturdy hotel laundry bags and hauled them along.

We sat on sofas and chairs along the walls of a large, well-proportioned room, and there she was, tiny, sturdy, squarish with broad cheekbones, round face, straight grey-black hair and eyes I couldn't stop looking at. One by one we were introduced to each other by our leaders.

Then came the presentation of our books. Because some of the books I had brought along were not my own, I felt they needed special explanation, so there I was, kneeling down and pulling them out of the bag and onto the low table. Ding Ling at first tried to make me stand up, but realized that I was kneeling for convenience, not only because of the low table and stack of books, but because with me kneeling and her sitting we were roughly face to face. Patrick told me later it was a marvelous sight; he felt there was an instantaneous bond between us. He could not have paid me a greater compliment. How I wanted to believe it. In spite of the naive terms in which they were conceived, Ding Ling has been in fact exactly the person of my early

111

fantasies. Only how much more impressive the reality of her life and work than my naive formulations could have envisaged.

Later, at the dinner during which the peking duck displayed something like twelve courses of glorious gustatory versatility, at the end of which a freshly roasted duck was brought in and carried from table to table to receive the applause of all who had just partaken of the inadvertent favours of its kind, I admit I slung back a "gambei" or two of sorghum alcohol in excess of my normal toasting measure. But everybody was kind. I was so obviously spaced-out by the experience they were probably relieved I wasn't swinging from the chandeliers.

It was her eyes. Ding Ling paid us the great compliment of inviting our group to tea at her home, where we met her husband, Ch'en Ming, and her lovely young student granddaughter. I was again drawn by those eyes. I kept thinking, "what stories she could tell me." What stories, what suffering endured, what understanding, what comprehension in those eyes. And sitting there in their modest and homey apartment, drinking tea and eating sweets, I suddenly realized why her eyes mesmerized me. The eyes of this seventy-six-year-old Chinese revolutionary feminist artist had the same expression my mother's eyes had had during the latter part of her life. It was as though I had finally dug my way through to China two years after my mother's death to find a message from her here. Something that both she and my mom knew and accepted permeated them, glowed from within their eyes. Let me get it right; it is not a shiny outward blaze, but inward, hot coal sensed through the ash, knowing simultaneously glow and heat and the burning that consumes and the ash of the already consumed, and accepting all as one. It is an inward expression but not a withdrawn one, not a turning away from the rest of us, but a soft human glow and yet a beyond-ness. What she knows! And further, to my astonishment, her husband, Ch'en Ming, has luminous deep brown eyes very similar to my dad's, though with soft curving folds covering the outer edges. I was so moved, I told them. For me it was more than just a meeting which gave me a strange sense of having encountered something of my parents again. It was a revelation of how mysterious and wonderful life can be. I could never have understood before that at the heart of revelation is mystery.

☯

WRITERS AND WRITING, SINGERS AND SONG

Most of the writers we met had been in some way traumatized during the Cultural Revolution. All were obviously concerned with how they were to use the time they had left, their newly re-won freedom to express, for the common weal. As Ding Ling was to say a few months later, to a group of scholars and students who had gathered to meet with her at York University in Toronto, "You must understand we are a collectivist society, and we will remain a collectivist society." Our meetings with the Chinese writers were in part attempts to come to understand what this implied in terms of literary work. In turn we tried to explain to them what we hold so dear, the freedom of expression we consider a supreme value in our society. We have none of us been subject to direct sanctions of the appalling order they described. In our society the means of suppression of what we disapprove of or do not want to acknowledge are both more haphazard and more sophisticated. We do not need to oppress openly in order to suppress. Keep the public taste happily debased and why do you need oppression? But how do we talk to the Chinese over such vastly different kinds of experience? They mistrust what they conceive to be our selfish coterie individualism, the subjective, neurotic, pessimistic, art for art's sake, the elitist concept of art for the few. How can we be any good if we have such small audiences? We, on the other hand, recoil at the thought that one of their biggest literary prizes hangs on the judgment of some four hundred thousand people.

We try to point out that the most popular selling writers on our continent are apt to be the ones who confirm people in the worst aspects of the culture, that our serious writers must take on the task, as Patrick declared, "to witness the world we're in with absolute truth," and what issues from this is not readily popular with people who are used to being helped to escape the implications of the premises by which they live. How can we then trust the mass taste?

Regarding our literary objectives, Gary talked of Canada as a new country. "We are the beginning of a new way of thinking, of looking at ourselves, of describing ourselves."

Pat Lane quoted Chairman Mao on "sharing" the world in peace between China, Russia and the U.S. Pat said that as a Canadian he did not want to be shared out among the larger powers, nor do other small lands. He talked about despair, and the value of a literature of despair, and said that by writing about it you change the world; the reflection of despair makes changes; people say we must see this does not happen again. He pointed out that a literature of hope can be a lie.

. Suzanne Paradis explained the special situation of the French in Canada, the ongoing problems out of which have emerged the disproportionate literary accomplishments of the Quebecois.

Alice Munro spoke of female experience and writing about it. She quoted Jean Rhys: "I write about myself because I am the only truth I know." She said of herself, with unselfconscious humility, "I work in the dark." She suggested that it is possible to be honest, to steer clear of oversimplifications and distortions, about "a writer's necessity to recognise and write about contradictions if she finds them."

Robert Kroetsch pointed out that the dominant literature in Canada isn't Canadian, it's American. U.S. advertising determines the value of a book. He spoke of the profit motive, and the brief, (one month) shelf life of a book. He spoke of serious writers among us as guerilla soldiers, of various traditions of story telling, of which the tall tale and the oral tradition are his

114

own. He told of his background, his father a farmer of virgin Canadian soil. He talked of story telling as a way of making ourselves human, and with characteristic gallantry, and possibly even with accuracy, of our women writers as heroic.

Geoff Hancock's survey of the literary magazines in Canada suggested the possibility that on a per capita basis, compared to those of a country with a billion people, the readership numbers might not, in fact, be that different.

As for me, I had brought along ten of the dolls my mother had made, and I showed them and talked about human creativity and waste and ageing and love for the children. I thought that whatever divides us, the dolls and my mother would remind us of the humanity we share.

Our hosts talked of their mistakes, of their suffering, of their passionate desire to learn, to find what they call "the correct line", to listen to the real voices of the people.

We did not, perhaps, convince each other completely, but we at least began to see that we must be willing to face each other in our own contexts if we are to begin to understand. Once we had brought our premises into the open we could confront each other right-side-up.

And the fun could begin. As one-to-one writers on a day-by-day basis we are a good deal closer than our abstractions would imply. Pat and Gary have been translating Chinese poetry and want to translate more, want to know what is being written, how it sounds, want to get some feeling for the quality of what is being written, as well as to hear the ancient writings sung. These evening sessions remain in my mind as some of the most unexpectedly joyous encounters of the whole trip: the poems and stories of our Chinese colleagues; Mr. Mao persuaded to read the striking four-line core of his prize-winning poem; and the young poet who had lost ten years in limbo during the Cultural Revolution, coaxed out of his shyness to read some of the ancient Sung poetry so Pat can get the feel of it; Pat's eyes closed, his head forward, listening with his entire body, and the young poet transformed; Suzanne Paradis at last persuaded to read in

115

French, insisting we all close our eyes; the sensation of poetry.

Above all, laughter, the laughter of Fan Baoci as she stood reading the Han poetry as her mother and grandmother had read it to her; laughter and the glad exclamations of our hosts as I showed some of mom's dolls; the extraordinary performance of Wang Ronghua when Alice and Bob would not read because they felt their stories were too long, and he proceeded to give an impromput recital of stories by each of them, in Chinese, with such verve and gusto that we were all carried away by the gaiety and dramatic flow of his narrative, and I ended up convinced I'd understood everything I'd heard.

Shared laughter, the ultimate healing art, brought even from me a couple of my rare bursts of rhythmic prose. Monkey helped me with this one:

WILD CANADIAN GEESE FIND MAGIC PLACE

In Xian
the Big Goose Pagoda
looks down
on a cedar fountain,
upside down
on a bamboo cloud
Its wind bells sing
cicadas in a courtyard
at noon

☯

**MORE MAGIC
FROM THE LONG DIG**

Yes, we were taken to The Great Wall, and I have the popsicle stick that climbed it with me, and shared the adventure of having briefly been a part of the only human-made object that can be seen from the moon.

I have also seen, most staggering sight of all, an army emerging from a giant grave. Near Xian we were taken to the huge quonset hut where eight thousand over-life size terra cotta soldiers, and their horses, in full regalia, are being separated from the soil in which they have been buried for some twenty two hundred years. They were created by order of Qin Shi Huang, the first Emperor of China, to guard one compass point of his tomb. There are said to be an equal number on guard at each of the other three compass points. This remarkable young tyrant, whose formidable exercise of will first unified China, is also reputed to have been dissauded by a courageous courtier from sending his own mother, when she displeased him, to work on the Great Wall. His central tumulus, filled no doubt with all manner of wonders, has not yet been excavated. The problem yet to be solved is how to preserve remains, which tend to disintegrate as did those in the Ming Tombs, on contact with the air. There is indeed something chilling about the emptiness of the Ming Tombs, where they say the final tableaux of death of emperors, and of concubines asphyxiated alive, disappeared, perhaps blessedly, before the very eyes of their discoverers, at the first puffs of air which entered those huge boxes in which their bodies had for so long been sealed. To reach the Ming Tombs you traverse a long road which is lined with magnificent guardian animal and human figures. The room-sized coffins themselves, however, in the great underground chambers, look like nothing so much as a huge piece of cubist sculptural art.

Wandering about that quonset hut, looking down at the several hundred superb clay people who have so far been excavated, as they stand arrayed in military formation, some on horse, some afoot, every single one different, each with his own face, his own unique expression, each a portrait, I couldn't get my jaw to shut. Thirty two thousand. The numbers are hard to conceive; they recede toward abstraction, drowned in innocuous, sandy-looking earth. Behind those already excavated

117

and reconstructed is a solid wall of loess, from which I can still see projecting, unforgettably, a single foot.

When I looked over the expanse of quiet ground, stretching as yet untouched toward the back of the hut, I saw a second group of soldiers, partially uncovered, some, to the waist, others with parts missing, pieces of human jutting from the soil, trapped in it, waiting with the patience we have been told by our hosts so often on this trip is the outstanding characteristic of the Chinese, for their release. Most striking of all, a section where only a partial layer of soil has been scraped away, and the faces, some still partly covered, some as though trying to push through, staring up from the earth in a tableau which could have illustrated Dante's humans trapped in the Inferno, or a Resurrection begun. I even had a momentary vision of myself, having persisted in my spade and fingernail direct route through middle earth, after 2200 years, emerging something like this.

Apparently, at various times during the centuries peasants have, in fact, accidentally unovered bits of these figures, but have thought them to be spirits and hastily retreated. One can imagine how the idea of spirits living just underground can become very deeply engrained in the popular culture over so many hundreds of years, with the whispered proof in fact so close to hand. In a sense the peasants were right after all; the timeless spirits were indeed waiting to re-emerge from the soil. For the Chinese it must be enormously heartening to think that whatever was endured in the names of tyrants and emperors it is these masses of marvelously executed figures of China's Everyman which finally emerge.

☯

A THRILL OF A FRILL:

Because of a shortage of hotel space, we had to give up the hope of seeing the famous limestone formations of Guilin, which appear so frequently in Chinese painting, jutting suddenly into the air unlike any mountains or hills you would normally imagine. And then, as though on this trip we are to be denied nothing, just as our plane is approaching Guangzhou, #6 Typhoon of the season blows up, and we are forced to fly to Guilin for a two-hour stopover, and see something of that extraordinary landscape after all. Somebody's been monkeying with the weather.

☯

FROM MY NOTES:

I have known only failed communists before, people who have spent their lives pushing boulders up hill, who have learned to perceive the act of standing still as a great step upward, inasmuch as it is at least not a step downward, or idealists who have become bitterly disillusioned, finally, with comrades who had apparently reached a level beyond them and were hurtling boulders back down at them. It is rather wonderful to meet people who have, for all their setbacks and errors, actually seen some positive results in the re-creating of their worlds. The older writers, those with the long stretch of memory, are a particularly moving group. They have survived invasions, occupations, revolutions, internecine struggles, external pressures, cultural upheavals. They have seen it all and know that in life there is always more to come. And yet there is something in them that is as young as new-born hope. Perhaps also, unlike so many of our aged, they still have the assurance that comes from knowing not only that they have earned their lives, but that they still belong in the world.

☯

VIGNETTE:

Our Guangzhou friends have got wind of the fact that Alice's birthday is coming up, so our first feast turns out to be a surprise birthday party. We're taken to a wonderful old palace overlooking the water, its decor beginning to show it has taken heavy use as the deservedly popular Half-Moon-Stream Restaurant. I will not go into great detail; suffice that according to Geoff's reckoning there were at least ten courses, seven in-betweens, three desserts. Highlights; a tray of hors d'oeuvres in the shape of a birthday basket, beautiful, with all kinds of deliciously unexpected things: the little gorgeous brown pears turn out to be rice flour stuffed with meat; quals eggs; a fish fried inside out that is scrumptious; a super soup called Spring-Melon-Clock, a speciality of the house, in which the soup with many meats is actually steamed in the melon, and Wang Ronghua gives me an uneasy thrill by asking if I can identify the many meats. I pass. There are longevity noodles for Alice, toasts with Cassia wine, poems, talk, laughter. Alice's response: "Since this is my fiftieth birthday, I'd like to invite you all to my hundredth." Instantaneous reaction from all of us, "We're coming!" With this gang it seems wholly possible.

☯

VIGNETTE:

Patrick is fascinated by the rituals by which people live. On the way to the hot springs near Guangzhou, our hosts stop the bus and get out at a roadside market, where farmers are squatting beside piles of melons and lychees, and weighing them for their customers on simple, hand-held scales. "Look how they're doing it!" Pat cries out suddenly. "I'm an old farmer, Adele. Do you know that in every country in the world farmers have a

different way of testing melons for ripeness? I want to see this."
For the next fifteen minutes or so I watch, and sneak a few
photographs, while Pat and our three friends, utterly absorbed,
palpate, knock, listen, feel the vibrations in their palms, exchange techniques, and finally, painstakingly and with due
ceremony, select the melons we will later be munching and slurp-
ing in hearting confirmation of the ancient wisdoms.

☯

VIGNETTE:

If, as I've heard people say, the apple that was so irresistible
to Adam and Eve was actually a date or a fig, then I begin to
suspect that the peaches that Stone Monkey stole in Heaven
were really Guangzhou lychee nuts in season. Picture huge
clusters of rich brown lychees with deep red overlay, the rough,
blush covered cheeks of nut-brown boys in summer. Inside,
moist, sweet, juicy glowing green flesh hugging a glossy
chestnut-dark kernel. Picture me, scoffing them down. Picture a
boat ride on a lovely green, dammed up lake, surrounded by
lushly covered hills of bamboo and pine, hills, we are told, that
were once stripped bare. We drink the ubiquitous orange squash
and stand in the open, on a raft-like appendage hooked to the
side of the boat, the better to enjoy the scene. Wei Qui had
fought the Japanese, and picked tea during the cultural
revoltuion. He described to one of my companions how, after
four years of it, whenever he sees a tea bush his fingers
automatically get ready to pluck, pluck the tender top leaves. He
would have been an opera singer had bronchial troubles not
turned him to writing. During our bus ride sing-songs he
demonstrates his love of Chinese Opera to us, as we exchange
cowboy songs and folk songs and protest songs, and songs Pat
wrote himself and every song we can think of turn-in turn-out

with ours hosts. On the raft, Wei Qui shows me he can infallibly select the juiciest lychees with the smallest nuts. I can still see his laughing face as Pat catches on, "Of course, the smallest lychees will have the smallest nuts."

☯

HEAVENLY LAKE:

China really looks like its paintings. From the Quang Tung Hot Springs Lodge, where we have been soaking in the healing waters, we drive along a winding narrow pink-yellow dirt road up a mountain, to where the water hangs and falls in numerous delicately rushing cascades. The ride reminds us of our Okanagan roads. I hold my breath and our cheerful young driver holds the horn around the hairpin turns. Along the cliff edges, to modify the bareness of the drop, cut bamboo is planted, and sprouts anew from its joints. Rusty cliffs, layered blue mountains, lush vegetation, green water, ornamented bridges, walks, rocks, more falls, more pools, the white stone goddess of the water, a lookout pagoda at the end of a slender causeway that juts into the delicious, soupy green water in which we swim, Heavenly Lake, where language and reality coalesce. If it had been called anything else would it have been such a divine experience? Or merely a pleasant swim in beautiful sur- roundings? There is magic in naming. I have swum in Heavenly Lake.

On our return the bus drops us not far from the spa and we chat and stroll along an avenue of eucalyptus, collecting bits of fragrant bark, which we learn is used to staunch bleeding. Our hosts point out what they think might be a relative of the Cana- dian maple, whose fame has apparently reached the Orient, because of the shape of the leaves and the fact that they too turn colour. We come on a stand of exquisite bamboo, golden, streaked with green. Yu Ru, who is a Southerner, learned a great deal about bambo when she was taught to draw as a youngster, which in itself is a suggestive bit of information about the teaching of art in China.

She was also the one usually sent by her family to the bamboo groves to select those ready for cutting. She tells us this type of bamboo, grown for display or ornamental purposes, is called "gold and jade." Once again I am struck by the use of naming as metaphor, and metaphor as reality. Naming here seems to be a way of extending and enhancing simultaneously the beauty and reality of things and ideas, by linking them together and making the abstraction essentially inhabit the thing, and things inhabit each other. I wonder if this tendency is due to a quality inherent in the language, and in the mode of thought of our hosts. I remember one of them insisting gently to me in Beijing that the Temple of Heaven, where the Ming Emperor prayed for good crops, actually was Heaven.

As we stroll and listen to Yu Ru's bamboo lore, I marvel again at the varieties of experience a life can emcompass. This same spare, slender lady, with the totally engaging smile that nearly every one of our group has independently mentioned to me, was actually there when the foreigners were finally kicked out of the posh island compound they had commandeered in Guangzhou. She immediately went in and selected the excellent location for the nursery we visited, where the children performed for us so irresistibly that Gary, already homesick for his kids, could hardly drag himself away, and declared he was ready to return to China not to teach in a University, but to work in a nursery. Here, as in the commune nursery where we were also delightfully entertained by the children, we reciprocated with their favourites, "Jingle Bells" and "Home on the Range."

By the time we gathered in Guangzhou again for our farewell banquet, I had sent Bi Shuowang, who first drew my attention to a stand of young bamboo, and talked of the place of the regal grass in the Chinese heart, my second outburst of song, in grateful response to the poem he had written separately on scrolls for each of us.

FOR MR. BI, RESPECTFULLY

Like broken bamboo
thrust into earth
my joints spring to life

Hot springs to ease
the bones' deep ache,
Kind words a dip
in Heavenly Lake

☯

FARING WELL:

There was a sense of special closeness at the final evening meal. Never did a feast feed more richly the human hunger for fabulous food and moving words. I remember one of our hosts remarking, "Poetry is the art of emotion, " and Patrick, "drunk on Cassia wine," borrowing my notebook and then and there writing his poem. "Against the Blue Curtain", inspired by the blue background against which Fan Baoci and I were sitting. And Huang Qingyun, who had seen so much since 1939, the year she had spent at Teachers' College in New York, murmuring, "Hunger makes poets." These are the best mementos; the living memories, the poems exchanged, the good talk, the poems written for us and given to us, beautifully written out in script, as feasts for the eyes as well as the heart.

Even as I write I pause to pick up a book, in English, called PEKING OPERA and MEI LANFANG, and I am sitting again in the ramshackle opera house. I had of course seen The Monkey King performed by the Peking Opera in Toronto a couple of years back. Now I am watching and listening to THE

DRUNKEN CONCUBINE. Lady Yang, favourite concubine of the Tang Emperor Ming Huang, has been stood up this evening in favour of her rival the Lady Mei. This Lady Yang, an actual historic personage, is said to have set the style in female beauty for many generations. Hers are the broad cheeks and elegantly swayed back we find so often in Chinese painting.

On the stage, the Dan, or female impersonator playing the exacting and exquisitely subtle role of the Lady Yang, is Mei Baoujiu, the son of Mei Lanfang, who first brought the role and the Peking Opera to the admiring attention of the world, in the nineteen thirties. Sitting beside me, apologising because he had been held up in traffic, and explaining story and performance of the works we are seeing to me step by step, is Mei Shaowu, also a son of Mei Lanfang, who co-authored this book about the Peking Opera and his illustrious father, which places this remarkable art form in the context of the other important dramatic theatres of our time. Afterwards we go backstage to meet the gifted actor, who may well be of the last generation of great female impersonators, since girls are now being trained for these roles.

Later on still, at the hotsprings outside of XiAn, where Chiang Kai Shek was ambushed by his own officers and escaped briefly, and reputedly without his teeth (how the detail humanizes), to the Pagoda on the cliffside where he was finally captured, we see also the sunken, mosaic tiled bath of Lady Yang. And finally in Hong Kong I even find a tape with Mei Lanfang himself doing THE DRUNKEN CONCUBINE.

During that final banquet in Guangzhou, when we tried to express our appreciation and our thanks to our hosts, I found myself speaking of the many patterns of fulfillment it had been my good fortune to experience during this journey, patterns which have in fact continued.

☯

JUNE 12, 1982 TRIUMPHANT EXIT THROUGH FOR-BIDDEN ENTRANCE

To Hong Kong. Our train passes through intensively cultivated terraced fields, with silver-buttocked water buffalo, the occasional humped brahma bull, orangey soil, lovely variegated greens, flooded rice fields, the landscape completely manicured by many hands, liberally sprinkled with people working, looking likes miles of formal garden, neat, clean, and so elegantly patterned. Here & there are grain-beating machines that work by treadle action, the worker pushing up and down with his foot to activate the machine which beats the rice from the straw which he then tosses aside to be tied and stooked in the shape of Chinese straw hats.

So this is what was hidden on the other side of those border hills I'd yearned towards in vain so many years ago, those hills which now begin to appear. As we travel through them I again see the hakka women in their black, fringed coolie hats, who inhabit this border region. As we approach the outer range I see that there are graves on this side of the scrim of hills as well as on the other side. It seems so strange to me to be emerging from The People's Republic to cross the bridge from which so many years before I had been turned away. It is a busy border crossing, changed and grown beyond recognition.

☯

Returning through Hong Kong is like being brought up too quickly after deep-water skin diving. The sudden change can give you the cultural bends. It is still a beautiful city in a beautiful setting, but it had changed a great deal in twenty-one years. Its heart is now encrusted with skyscrapers like that of any large Western city.

In the short time we were there we were rooked by taxi sharks, and both Geoff and I had our bags razor-slashed. One evening we walked around the Peak on Victoria Island, which looks down on the gorgeously illuminated brocade of the city. Afterwards, we descended and found a Malaysian restaurant. We had just finished a very tasty meal, when I noticed a sleek, fat black sausage of a rat, about nine inches long, with about the same length of tail, making his leisurely way up the wall in front of my eyes and onto the patterned dropped ceiling which provides him, and presumably his family, with a complete set of rat-walks. For the first instant, jovial and filled with food, I was about to call the proprietor's attention to his "pet", when I suddenly realized what I was looking at.

In the plane crossing the Pacific they were still showing the same banal situation comedy they had been showing when we set out. We were on our way home.

☯

RECOGNITION: THE TWO-WAY ROAD TO CHINA

When life is being generous it can be prodigal in generosity beyond what we dare hope. A few months after our return from China we had the pleasure of welcoming Ding Ling and Ch'en Ming to our own country. Margaret Laurence joined the Old China Hands in co-hosting their stay in Ontario, and we tried, for the all-too-brief period of their visit, to show them something of our country and how we live. The road to China runs both ways, after all, and it seemed to me that the visit with which they honoured us was a continuation of my own journey and developed yet further the patterns of fulfillment of which I have been speaking. At a luncheon banquet which was given in their honour by the Chinese Community of Toronto, Ding Ling and Ch'en Ming were presented with a powerful painting by a talented young Chinese Canadian artist, Hing Mak. They wanted our guests to take back something which would tell of the lives of the early Chinese immigrants to this country, and, particularly for Ding Ling, which would tell of the lives of the women. The woman in the painting is bent over a sewing machine, in the dim light. At the same time as she is sewing she is rocking her child with the bare foot which she has hooked under its cradle. Somehow, in the bold, strong strokes one can feel the long hours, the double work, the anxious, divided attention. I was startled and moved by the painting. Its subject was so familiar to me. It is the story of my mother's life as an immigrant too.

When it was time to see Ding Ling, Ch'en Ming, and their attentive factotum, our magician Richard Liu off, I had run out of party clothes, and appeared at the airport in my more usual pants and parka. Ch'en Ming knows some English, but Ding Ling's glad cry of recognition, when she saw me, was uttered in the first and only English words I heard her speak. "Far-mer!" she cried. Then, with a proud sweep of her arm, she pointed to herself. "Me too!"

That's how to go to China.

My Own China

by Suzanne Paradis

I did not really believe it
it seemed so much the unrolling
of an incredible dream.
            (Gary Geddes, *Letter of the Master of Horse*)

Quand j'aurai le temps, j'irai à Paris,
j'irai en Grèce ou en Chine...
            (A song of mine, written in 1970)

Should I keep silent about the three months of incredulity and
disbelief following the first phone call from Gary Geddes, the
instigator of that trip to China? Perhaps, but so much do these
words exactly describe the climate in which that sumptuous and
unexpected invitation has drawn and submerged me, between
March 23 (Would you like to go to China?) and June 28
(Tomorrow, Dorval airport, departure at 10h30 for Vancouver).
Besides, there will be time enough to insist on that other state of
stupor and wonder and to explain the extreme fervour with
which I experienced my very first encounter with a live China,

the one not to be found in books or world maps. New China? Popular China? Communist China? A China ambiguous and saddened by our preconceptions?

No. A China made to measure for me, unknown motherland of a large part of my imagination; the one whose silence and sensuality surround you so deeply that you can only give in to its seduction. Although I did consult with my family on March 23, had I not already left for that China, without consulting anyone, especially not my own self? The daily routine was already disturbed, a large smoke screen covering and refreshing it; unfolding junks and pagodas lost in endless clouds floating about.

Nonetheless three days later I would say *yes,* encouraged by my sons spreading out maps, encyclopedias, magazines and folders gathered from their bedrooms (of course, the whole world fits, in loose leaf form, within their umpteen drawers), from the airport and travel agencies. *I did not really believe it!* So I had to keep on dreaming until the shapings of the fabulous moment would become familiar and real. I am not afraid of fiction; but such an incredible reality, a land suddenly flooding from all shores into my consciousness, for its dikes have been severed by a phone call, that it brings up in me a reflex of self-defense. See China, very well! But not to be blinded by a vision that would have to fit within reason in record time. Dream of China? Is it not the means by which any reality was ever tamed? Let the continent open up before the true rising sun...

I admit I lost my footing at least once a day for three months. My Chinese dream could vanish at any question. One cannot bring China into one's bedroom without forcing the doors a bit, without strange vibrations to the walls and, on practical grounds, without breaking the daily rhythm already perturbed at the coming of vacation.

Should I also give some importance to the very date of June 29 where I played a flying Tom Thumb because of a late flight? When I had to combine both the talents of Mary Poppins and Peter Pan to collect my airplane ticket at Dorval, my passport

130

and visa in Vancouver and my six travelling companions in Tokyo... the day after our rendez-vous in Vancouver? Where I boarded flights between Montreal, Toronto, Vancouver, Los Angeles (Hi! Messrs Bell and Doucet, from Arvida!), Honolulu and, at last, Tokyo, adding almost enough flight time required to become a pilot? I give such importance to that endless and odd mileage because it has helped keep me for several more hours in the state the poet has described as *the unrolling of an incredible dream*. That wild race above the earth was bringing me closer to China, even more surely than the quiet trip planned. That is to say, I was mentally ready, my mind receptive much before landing in China.

So it was in Tokyo, Narita airport (and not Anheda where I arrived in early morning) that I joined the group, finding out names and physical identities: novelist and drama creator Adele Wiseman, novelist Alice Munro, poet Patrick Lane, poet and novelist Robert Kroetsch, Geoffrey Hancock, editor of the *Canadian Fiction magazine,* and Gary Geddes poet and editor, and organizer of our trip. Their sudden presence, although long awaited, changed this multitudinous airport into a cool oasis and brought abruptly the rupture with the West. Already Adele, Alice, Pat, Bob, Geoff and Gary are within myself, an intimate part of my China, and I will get to know them through this particular filter, unforgettable and infinitely precious.

In a few hours, we will be in Beijing. I have not really stretched out for two days; the layover in Shanghai will plunge us into the humid and comfortable heat in all of China from North to South. Our status as guests of the Chinese Writers' Association will render straightforward all our moves, formalities and living adjustments. We will be met, spoiled, taken to each airport. In Chinaland during our ten day stay, we will benefit from the refined and generous hospitality of our Chinese colleagues: hotels, meals, transportation, the thousand and one services required by our presence amongst them, no detail was left out pertaining to our comfort and amazement. Of course Chinese hospitality is gay and affectionate, well prepared to please the

131

poets and children that we are, that we become from hour to hour, gliding on the irresistible descent I must call euphoria, when the time will come to put into words my emotions and feelings.

To awaken in Beijing, in that hotel with a symbolic name, the Friendship, was it not as amazing as my wondering space excursion between the two continents? Balanced between the unusual and the real which here, for bewildered visitors, constitute the one and only reality, we made our way, blowing the car horn, across the incoming tide of a crowd of people, some on foot, some on bikes, a tide carrying the deepest fascination on mind and senses. We faced the wondrous opposites of both the modern and ancient of that city in construction, with imperialistic depths, kilometers outside the memory palaces, statues and carved columns, temples, slums and new buildings, overflowing with a huge population; the most gigantic eye-cheater ever meditated by yesterday's man to the intention of tomorrow's. We were grabbed by that velvet fist, initiated, changed, placed defenseless in that second state of mind where poets raised, from the confidence of the universe, the never heard secrets that haunt them.

Oh the mountains of Beijing, their iron peaks girdled with Laurentide green velvet, their walls half crumbled, their reddish stone, their appletrees, peachtrees, cedars and apricot trees, hollyhocks and straw hats, brown swallows and small horses hitched by two, three or four to antique racks loaded with rocks or soil! Countryside sad and ragged of Beijing, with fields of cucumbers and tomatoes, donkeys and ducks, pine trees, sheep, corn and ponies, the ugly and discolored soil of the North. Beijing the great, the crowded, the desolate queen of palaces and slums inhabited by the same magic... Beijing drives into you, not insidiously, but with the extraordinary openness and the gaiety of China in early morning, active, dreamy, quite daring behind its spontaneous laughter and its dizzy quietness.

132

Five important meetings with members of the Writers' association took place during the ten day stay in China. On July 2, first contact of our delegation and the Chinese directors, of which Ding Ling, famous Beijing writer who would the next day do us the honor of inviting us to her home. The climate which would prevail all during our stay is already established: a warmth, an amazement (we constitute the very first delegation of western writers to be welcome into new China), an openly shared emotion and pleasure. Our ignorance concerning one another, instead of being an obstacle to a coming together, becomes a springboard to our curiousity and that of those facing us.

On July 3, our hosts will tell us about their literature, answering our questions and describing the horrors of the regime initiated by the *Band of the Four* which reduced to silence most writers. Bubbling eyes, high pitched speech, the writers will express the joy at recovering a portion of their freedom. Some will explain the panegyric of the Party and the communist regime; but we will quite often hear of a still existing form of censorship for the Chinese writer. Do not his writings belong automatically to the people which inspires them? The modern writer's vocation is dual faceted. On one side, he wishes to give his country a personal view corresponding to reality as understood by him. On the other side, he is asked to build up the people's hope and confidence, by smoothing out the truth if necessary.

The extreme and permanent intimacy in which the Chinese live shows how uncertain notions of individual freedom are. Even after only one day in Beijing, I could hardly propose as a concrete ideal what, for example, Virginia Woolf would define as a room of ones own. Individual rights are necessarily those of the masses, and China keeps on dreaming patiently and seriously: it will come out of its misery (hunger, ignorance, unemployment, unhealthy and scarce lodgings, national isolation). The end could well justify the means, and it would be folly to offer short-sighted judgments on the present processes.

So much so, that the facts stated by the Canadian writers, on July 4, forced a reflection on the assembly of the writer's condition in a capitalistic society, lacking neither resources nor vital space. Each one of the members of our delegation did present an outlook on the Canadian literary universe, and I had the frightening privilege of bringing out my own views on the situation prevailing in Quebec.

Except for Alice Munro, whose resumé took in the mysteries and contradictions of the literary experience, mostly feminine, and the importance of offering an authentic and personal view of the world; and Adele Wiseman, who praised spontaneous and versatile creativity of the human being placed in conditions favorable to inspiration and work (and that, with the help of a showing of marvellous dolls created by her mother); every speech would touch upon the social and political implications of Canadian and Quebec literature.

My own exposé brought back to mind the *Grande Noircoeur,* the October crisis, the referendum and a large number of small and great events which built Quebec history and literature. And could Gary Geddes avoid the shadow of the two solitudes while describing the Canadian reality? Certainly Patrick Lane could not have denied the very real possibility of separation of the Western provinces, saddled to the dream of sovereignty noisily persuaded by Quebec for the last twenty years. Despite the nasty looks of all America not even Bob Kroesch could have remained silent about the pressure exerted by the United States on the survival of Canadian books. The creative work, in Canada as in Quebec, subscribes to a neverending fight to maintain balance between the artist's great temptation to speak on in complete freedom, and the pressures placed on him by the national and the general expectations of readers. Geoffrey Hancock, who is the editor of his own magazine from coast to coast, gave further evidence of that delicate balance.

To see China and to live. The sentiment I feel is the opposite of death, an overabundance, the attention of the gods; but with such intensity that I lose control of my senses. My own thoughts do not reach me. Temple of the Sun, Great Wall of China where I climb as to reach heaven, without any tiredness or impatience, quite alone in a crowd, at the heart of a wordless poem. The Ming tombs and their sorcerer's writings. The Summer Palace, blue and green floating in the soft shadows of the sun. Pagodas. Xian gardens, giant lotuses opening in the night, planetrees, weeping willows, crickets in stereo sound. Oh Xian and the diffused spirit of Confucius! I wish nothing but to see, touch, smell, listen, bathe in an ocean of ignorance, with no desire to learn, vividly mingled to that greyish soil, to the galleries, to that captivating heat and ageless tombs...

What serenity in these shrines incubated by the gods, haunted by souls liberated by death into earthly refuges. I am bewildered. But this dizziness operated at a given rhythm within myself. It does not push around. It does not frighten, as an act of love duly prepared, forcing the agreement of each sense, wrapping up, preventing all leave. My resistance is absorbed, rendered absolutely illogical and artificial. Is this death? For me, it is the Absolute, in an aura of extreme and profound sensuality. My soul opens up, stretches out, takes leave of all frontiers that held it prisoner. It reaches to universal poetry, to that eternity where tigers and lotuses endlessly meet...

And to live. All that would be mirages and lies, a sort of fabulous cinema: the blinding of Guangzhou vegetation, the bouncing silence of the night of the crickets, the exquisite food of our friendly meals, the infinite joy of a fulfilled body. And everywhere, the ever attentive and discrete presence of our Chinese brothers and sisters. And what can be said about the powerful provocation of the surroundings, the distilled enchantment of a thousand secret voices?

From time to time, we would escape, but to find ourselves

back into another area of the same dream: Gary playing the guitar and singing in a Beijing backstreet; Patrick dancing a jig to the people's delight; Ding Ling astonished because I kiss her instead of shaking her hand, at the door of her apartment; the moving tenderness of small children, so beautiful we could never resist the temptation to speak to them, to touch them, to sing for them. And the goodbye meals in Beijing, in Guangzhou... the partings...

No doubt I do not know China (who could boast such knowledge even after months of living there?). Perhaps I only came close to Her, throughout a marvellous love story. She, the infinitely multiple and mysterious, such that the most daring dream could barely imagine. She bore into the deep tissue of my flesh, unforgettable, generous, magnificent. She has not changed my life, but much more: my very soul. She is not a part of my memory but a part of my blood.

☯

It is in Hong Kong, where we spent the last three days of our trip, that I realized how spoiled I had been. Why me?

Hong Kong the noisy city, nervous, hallucinatory; Hong Kong the cosmopolitan, at the edge of China but turning its back on Her. Surprisingly, Hong Kong proved to be the most favorable milieu for a reply to my question.

What had I gone there for? In answer to an unbelievable invitation, as it happens more and more often in my otherwise quiet writer's life? No. Even if I owe to a conspiration of the stars, a most fanciful star-system, the privilege of taking part in this trip. To take a vacation? I always spend summer in Quebec. To kill time? I am always running short of time.

In all frankness, I went to my rendez-vous to the end of the world blindly willing and frightened to death. But a fortnight was enough to copy my heart and soul after those of China, eternal.

From now on I have only to close my eyes for there to burst

out, in hardly bearable push, many images, lights, scents and sounds; for my skin and bones recapture the sumptuous and silent elasticity of desire. I can never go back to China; it is no longer possible, for I am there and there will remain. My own China.

*These two words translate the political regime of Prime Minister Maurice Duplessis (1936-1959): censure, choking of cultural and artistic values, loathing of intellectual objectives. The painter Paul-Emile Borduas replied to Mr. Duplessis by the publishing of a declaration: *Le Refus global* (1948).

The universe holds into a single hand
shaken with all its strength
willows fall
and the weeping soul of the poplars

Beijing July 1981

Soft eyes of the sun
transfusion of sweat and desire
into a single offering
limp hours slip off my back and are crushed
desire has tiger's teeth and tears at time

Wild eyes of the sun
not to love even when flesh cries out
and the soul is nothing but a frozen brook

Beijing July 1981

Keen hearth of daybreak
lotus and mandarins
peaches ripening in the mountain

there are no stars
the moon has been pregnant for over a thousand years

I am a drop of water
and eternity knows not of me

Beijing July 1981

Why bones in the shadow of my flesh
and needlefuls of blood embroidering my breath
flame red and sulphur
and golden bunches
in fields of dead wheat

Beijing July 1981

I know not what magic creates
words hardly have time to awaken
that they go back to sleep
here they have nothing to say

Beijing July 1981

Raise your eyes
to earth level
shadow has a thousand hiding places
into each opening of daytime
for every hour of loneliness and absence
none missing

Beijing July 1981

The cedar no longer numbers its darts
it climbs to the top of the sky
the dark moon opens a passage
as to gatherings of unmoving birds

at that distance
I hardly distinguish the target
that has not yet begun to die

Beijing July 1981

Let us not wait
for the moon to move to the next quarter
the roundness of night goes to the head
with a honey soul to seduce

let us hold that dizziness at hand

Beijing July 1981

The river runs invisible
even with the pines light
I have never known so vivid a wait
so slow a leafing

not a bark in the whole city
not a single shadow of animal
the river travels through the pine-cones

Beijing July 1981

Fresher mountains
dissolve morning
the air lightens and rises a deafer
breeze

silence crosses my voice
and the sun's sharp rays tear at flanks
of desire.

Xian July 1981

The old city crumbles
its stones have loosened the tightening of centuries
the river has tamed its bridges
and turned over its bed so to sleep

quietly a man gathers rocks
before they turn to dust

Xian July 1981

There is a star every night
that collects the light of day
the whole world's brightness
and whirls over the mountain
to the nearest dawn

the sunrise can only come from that star
that finds light again from the beginning

Xian July 1981

Time has all the rainbow's colors
its eyes burn and shine
beads mirrors small jade buddhas
a two-cent-prayer comes out of the music box
a child with almond shaped eyes is older by a day

I slip into a bottomless age
youth

Xian July 1981

the sky has two holes one for the moon
the other for the sun
it sleeps in peace and balance
between their flames
it has a thousand small silver eyes
to spy in their fool's games

Xian July 1981

Children sing and bring joy
they withdraw their tears from the sun
like so many sparkles

bunches of smiles so white that one dreams

building again this world
to gain time unto eternity

we could say the same of the sea

Hong Kong July 1981

Horses pass by in the wind
the sun blooms
from their diamond hoofs

and great crazy planets
build a tan from their shadow

Hong Kong July 1981

I am leaving with sea all around
with two big white cargos
one for the rain the other for tomorrow

Hong Kong July 1981

First Trip to China

by Geoff Hancock

Flying over the warm, grey clouds of Shanghai, I begin my transformation. I am no longer an Aries, born in 1946; I am a Chinese, born in the Year of the Dog, and my flower is the cherry blossom. Fields emerge from the clouds as the plane drops lower, and I feel the ring in my hands as I slip the choker around the cormorant's throat on my sampan home. Within minutes I add 5,000 years to my life. Screeching wheels, lurch of brakes, and we are on the ground. A plane, an airport, a strange humid twilight. The red characters on the terminal building are the ideogram for 'Shangai Airport'. What could be simpler? And yet, when I step off this plane I know I will step into a China that is far from simple, that will require constant redefinition.

At the foot of the ramp, a teenage soldier stands in the half-light, holding a submachine gun. He wears blue trousers, a jacket of army khaki without insignia. The light turns to purpling darkness. He looks at me as I rush past, appraising. I feel naked — so much for my sampan and cormorant, my 5,000 years.

Passport control. Other soldiers, young men and women,

laugh among themselves and apply the precious stamp. Our names mean nothing to them and will mean progressively less to us from now on. The naming and unnaming has begun, as Kroetsch said in Tokyo when I received the title 'Serpent with One Fang'. Strange fact, but I remember the taxi driver during that ride looking at us through the rear-view mirror — he wore white gloves.

Inside the Shanghai terminal building is an unexpected ad for liquor. A Great Wall of Cognac, to keep out barbarous thoughts. Flickering lights of uncertain wattage. The humidity makes everything wilt in our hands. A rush of other tourists assaults the gift shop for paper fans, silk robes, jade grapes. I join the line for currency exchange, pushing like the others for my share of the 'people's' money. Soon we are toasting each other with warm beer, which the Chinese consider healthier than cold beer, and are posing uncomfortably for a group photograph.

We are not where we expected to be and there is still a long haul before we reach the isolated northern capital of Beijing. But we are here at last, in China, and it is enough.

Several of our hosts, members of the Chinese Writers' Association, meet us at the airport in Beijing. We grin from ear to ear as we are introduced. Our translators, Madame Fan Boaci, and Mr. Wang Ronghua are to accompany us around China. Their effortless translations dispel all worry about the impossibilities of communication between different cultures. With Mr. Bi, the jovial, stout, spokesperson, poet, photographer, we adopt the ritual of applauding each other as we are introduced. Here is Patrick wearing his furled up cowboy hat; Adele has a suitcase so heavy the hinges have broken; Alice looks fresh and cool as a morning marketplace, despite people staring at her painted toenails: Bob, the great white buffalo, roars and snorts, pawing the ground, waiting for everything to be deconstructed and reinvented; Gary, the ideal tour leader, with a gift for rhetoric and diplomacy; Suzanne, lost for two days because of a bad airport connection, already making

147

enough notes to complete a couple of books; and Hancock, so beside myself with excitement I am my own doppleganger, taking notes, tape recordings, and photographs of a China that refuses to stand still.

It takes about an hour to get from the Beijing Airport to the Russian built Friendship Hotel on the edge of the city. On this sultry summer evening, the first of July, along a straight road lined with willow trees and illuminated with pale orange street lamps, we race along in an airconditioned Toyota bus. The driver honks furiously, although no cars are in sight. Drivers can lose their license if an accident occurs. We pass a few farm trucks, which are driving only with parking lights and at least a dozen farmers in the dumper, standing at attention, smiling, holding rakes and hoes. Patrick points out to Robert, both prairie boys now, how three horses are hitched together to pull the cart, the lead horse to the curb side so he won't swing into traffic. Scrawny horses too. Puttering along the road are strange motorized tractors, coughing black smoke from one horsepower engines. People sit by the curbs on low wooden stools, and fan themselves. Every hundred metres or so, a group half across the road amuses itself with dice, checkers, or bei-fan, a sort of poker minus the gambling. All Chinese games. In their deft moves lies the kinship between ancient and modern China.

I feel the closeness of village life. The earth has a stronger gravity here, pulling the bus closer to the road. Water hyacinths, buffalo, peanuts, farmers on bikes press against the window. No guidebook can prepare you for the rice paddies of China. I look out the window; with a little shock of recognition, I feel the mud and straw and water around my ankles and wrists as I pull a handful of green rice shoots loose from the paddy with a squelching sound.

I'm glad we are entering Beijing at night. I know the city is vast, dusty, much under construction. New apartment complexes, roads, great drainage ditches appearing to be built by hand, festooned with bamboo scaffolding, some still with tree branches on top to deceive evil spirits into thinking they are

148

passing over a forest. At night, though, those things are scarcely visible. Tomorrow will be soon enough for such things. Now there are other surprises in store for us in Beijing. The beauty of the pagodas on the train station, trimmed with lights. The stillness of the streets, broken occasionally by sudden squawkings, of geese, or a flock of sheep being herded down a sidestreet. And at our hotel, a bigger surprise. On the rooftop terrace, French and African exchange students have installed streamers of coloured lights, and a stereo system. Disco has arrived in old Peking. I think of Toronto rock musician, B.B. Gabor, whose hit single "Nyet, Nyet, Soviet" might find appropriate airplay here. We toast ourselves again, with big bottles of warm beer.

In our rooms, a television. But my room has no electric socket. As for the cockroaches, Patrick says: "Ah, they're just the little guys." A reminder of the lobster sized roaches I have seen in a hotel room in central Brazil. For me the bigger treat is the flowered tea thermos, a little packet of jasmine tea, and teacup with lid. But my hopes of a silk bedspread are dashed. The quilt is acrylic.

Perhaps because of the excitement, or crossing the international date line, dawn, the first morning in China, arrived early, bringing with it the twittering of thousands of swallows which emerge from beneath the cornices of the hotel. I tape them, and even at 5 a.m. I can feel what the Chinese call the tiger's heat of July beginning to stir.

I go to a courtyard behind the hotel, which stands on a complex of several acres. The Chinese are fond of grottoes and rockeries, and large mishappen stones stand next to trees parched by a two year drought. In their ugliness and emptiness, so the Chinese say, lies their beauty, their strength, their natural creative forces. In China, all objects are flooded with meaning.

But my inspiration comes from tai chi. Early risers perform in slow motion, some empty-balanced, some with tasseled swords. This soft internal art balances the yin and yang forces of the constant energy flow within the body. I am fascinated by the

149

martial arts and have studied kung fu before American ser-
vicemen brought the martial arts back from Vietnam, or before
the popularity of Bruce Lee movies. I am magnetically drawn to
a sunlit glade where a master swordsman does his forms. Not
with a wooden sword, but with the real thing, a tassel attached
to the hilt. He does his forms with tremendous speed. With one
mistake, his arms would be entangled by the tassel, and a serious
injury could result. But he does not err.

This glade, with its streams of sunlight, brings back a
strange feeling. A memory of some other glade? When I might
have been a Chinese warrior, perfecting my kung fu and arguing
about which is the correct style? Hung Gar with its deadly one
inch punches. Wing Chun with its eagle claws, and swift kicks
perfectly adapted for close fighting in alleys or bars. Shaolin
style, named after the famed fighting monks who battled the
Manchu invaders in the 17th century, their lethal moves based
on animal forms.

I am in touch with some hidden part of myself. Remember-
ing how a preying mantis move can paralyse an arm; where the
white-ape-reaching-for-a-cup-of-wine becomes a choke hold;
where two-dragons-groping-for-pearls gouges the eyes. My arms
as snakes, hands as snake heads, coiled to strike out an oppo-
nent. The force of redirected energy in the art of breaking —
boards, bricks, blocks of ice, bones — made me as enthusiastic
as Li Po's wildest fantasies after drinking wine. One punch·
smashes the Yellow Crane Pavillion, one kick overturns the Par-
rot Island.

☯

In China, we were always off balance. Every picture in
China had a meaning, every image led inward to a philosophy,
or legend, fairy tale, or story. A bowl, a teacup, a wide porcelain
spoon, a paper lantern had a story behind it. A poem. We were
completely surrounded by Chinese literature. Little wonder that
we began to change. Gary said he was doing a lot of

psychological house-cleaning. Kroetsch looked as if he belonged sitting on a stylized horse on the "spirit road" of the Ming Emperors. By the time we arrived at the Great Wall, I could peer through the perfectly detailed arrow slits and look across the brown distance for the pale dust of a distant rider. With hot wind from the steppes at my back, I had time to light my signal fire. Standing on the Great Wall, looking over fallen stone, with grass growing in the masonry, feeling what the Chinese must feel.

I had to move from *my* Canada to *this* China. Yet, this country has a scale of one mile to the mile and its map cannot be unfolded. At home I had known a different China. Where truck farmers wore straw hats bent over hoes, between row of beans, peas, tomatoes, radishes, and lettuce on Lulu Island. I know of corner greengrocers, herbalists, restauranteurs with secret recipes for barbecued pork. I brought with me, images of Vancouver's Chinatown. Pender, Main, Gore and Powell streets, where dragon dancers at Chinese New Years leapt amidst exploding firecrackers. Rows of old men reading the pages of the *Chinese Times* taped inside the publisher's window. But in Canada, we were 'lo fan' — white devils — and to understand Chinese required more than mastery of a few phrases and numbers.

What we know always gets in the way. The gravitational pull of the west lowers a window of resistance in front of my eyes. At first I disliked the unfamiliar about China. Their yellow soft drink, served warm, and with sediment at the bottom. Saucers of garlic cloves which the Chinese serve as we would salt peanuts. I was afraid of misunderstanding China, of running out of energy, of travelling with a group of Canadian writers, of making speeches. I didn't want to get blind drunk on cassia wine. I felt trapped — I see that now — in my Canadian routine, diet, and sleep patterns. I sipped a Coca-Cola, imported from San Francisco, and ignored the Chinese imitation, "Heavenly Cola". I refused to let go and fly into the larger orbit of Chinese life.

But that was to change. That tight hold upon routine began

151

to relax. And what marked the change? Suzanne, embracing an entire nursery of five year old children? A deeper awareness of world history? The Chinese, after all, traded silk with Rome in the second century, B.C., carrying the bolts on two humped camels along the Great Silk Road fifteen centuries before Marco Polo's epic journey the other way. Or was it learning from Gary that the Chinese discovered North America in the fifth century A.D., nearly five hundred years before the Vikings, by landing on the Pacific Coast, possibly around Vancouver. My map of China, and my map of myself, were filling themselves in. New roads were there to be followed.

Suddenly all the statistics managers had given us about the model commune, the hydro electric factory, the silk factory, the firecracker factory, hinted at some larger narrative. China could be anything we wanted it to be. Encouraged to eat 300 lychee nuts a day, juicy as spring, I began to feel, as did Paul Eluard in some other place, that the horizon was unknotting its belt for us. When the Chinese kids sang to us, about Tianeman Square in the spring, we sang back: "Jingle Bells," or "Alouette." We were beginning to define ourselves.

I was fascinated by the Chinese imagination at work. The highest praise an artist could receive was to be told he painted a horse or an insect as if he were a horse or an insect. Because I felt close to the Chinese imagination, every work of painting, sculpture, porcelain; every pagoda, garden, temple; each piece of bronze, carving, jewellery, unfolded, as the Buddhist Diamond Sutra describes life, 'like a dream, like a vision, like a bubble, like a shadow, like dew, like lightning'.

Within half a day in China, I was immersed in new metaphors. The Temple of Heaven, until the Chinese revolution of 1912, was once the most sacred place in China. It was seen only by the emperor and his priests. The complex, surrounded by three and a half miles of wall, is a stone metaphor for heaven and earth. Square buildings are associated with earth. Some are even converted into souvenir stands. While round buildings are associated with heaven. The boundary between them is an archway with stone clouds, and to step through this simple gateway into a courtyard filled with pink rhodedendrons, is to leave earth behind.

But ironically, not too far behind. In a courtyard of the temple, where Chinese tourists pose for photographs, they stand beside a new model automobile. They pose by the car as if it were the most sacred of objects. (Curiously, in the lobby of Hamilton Place, I had seen the same thing: Canadian tourists gawking at a power equipped American car.) Where the emperor was once carried in a sedan chair, busloads of tourists now walk. Old gentlemen stroll with their bird cages, young women push bamboo baby buggies. Japanese tourists huddle together, carrying plastic flight bags and snapping pictures of each other.

But heaven was just a step away, and proof that the circle is the great central fact. I'm glad I live in a world where not all mystery is exhausted. When the emperor of China spoke a prayer for the good harvest of his people, he spoke from the Altar of Heaven. His voice travelled over eight hundred yards from the small stone circle in the centre of the altar, vibrated upon the tip of the triple roofed Temple of Heaven, travelled throught its windows trimmed with green and gold, and back through the earth in an arc that ended at the emperor's feet. The Temple of Heaven is an invisible globe resting upon the earth. To be on this earth and to experience the invisible became the essence of the Chinese experience for me. I stood on the Altar of Heaven and spoke. My voice echoed back, entered through my feet, and shot up through the roof of my head like a rocket going to heaven.

The cause of this acoustical phenomenon is a series of stone pillars, nine in all, arranged equidistant around the perimeters of the circle. They are so precisely arranged that a speaking voice creates a simultaneous echo at the source. But the effect is at once aggressive, yet dreamlike.

We had not learned that the real China, however, lies between the blockbuster sights our guides were so eager to show us. If the Heaven suggested to us was at once a moral principle and a mandate for each dynasty, each new emperor, the earthly forms of the Forbidden City which we next visited provided the greatest architectural symphony in the world. In a guidebook, the palaces appear as well organized as the peasant huts which served as the original models. But to move from the diagram to the actual place is to move from the score to the symphony. Fortunately, we had been fortified by an excellent eight course lunch, where we had taught Suzanne to use chopsticks. Energy is needed when confronting a different kind of logic, where my own sense of art and history could find no comfortable place to rest.

The Forbidden City is both a historical relic needing repairs, and a dreamed experience hinting at buried secrets and a clamourous past. The practical and the poetic mingle together. A cornice simultaneously echoes the curve of a pine branch, fools passing demons, and keeps rainwater away from the walls. It also serves as a perch for the guardian spirits. There are usually nine of them, baking in the blistering sun of July. We purchased cheap straw hats to keep ourselves from frying in the heat, and I shaped mine into a fashionable 1930s fedora. A hint, perhaps, of some secret in my past.

·Our bus raced through the main entrance, through the Imperial Gate at the south entrance, beneath the immense portrait of Mao Zedong. The driver honking furiously as usual; visitors and workmen scampering out of the way. The Forbidden City, now known as the Palace Museum, rapidly began to unfold its series of walled palaces, each set inside the other. But unlike the Temple of Heaven, here, exploration was dependent upon movement. The ninety palaces of the Ming Emperors are a complex labyrinth, with 9,000 rooms, dragons everywhere, the reddish walls symbolizing the auspicious North Star. My recollection afterwards was that the palaces shimmered. Though we walked half an afternoon, and I photographed everything in sight, the actual experience cannot easily be conveyed. Can I convey the essence of Beethoven's Ninth Symphony with a picture of the orchestra?

Like the correspondences of Baudelaire, each aspect of the Imperial Palace is supposed to lead us from the physical world into a correspondence with the spiritual. The actual world reflects, and then leads us, to the other. For a place so immense, so physical, the real effects are hallucinatory. One palace gave way to another. Courtyards mingled with staircases. Each palace a modest variation on the one preceding it. Changing, shimmering, like a film montage, the gold roofs.

The gold roofs! I wallowed in the gold, snapped photos until I ran out of film. I felt the power of the imperial colour, yellow, which since the 13th century was associated with the Ming emperors. Each yellow tile had five glazes, which corresponded to the Five Jewels of Buddha, and the five directions: north, east, west, south, and centre. The emperor comes from the centre of the universe.

"Like the zen of pottery," I said to Patrick, "the glaze forms a barrier between the real and the spiritual."

"A line of poetry should do the same thing," he replied.

I began to change again in the Forbidden City. I began to see my comrades in a different way. Our group, straggling across a courtyard with as many as five translators for the seven of us. There was Madame Fan, sunhat in place, explaining something to Alice. Adele, the lens cap still on her camera, photographing iron cranes, symbols of longevity. Patrick stands, his cowboy hat off, next to a giant bronze yuan, or dragon/tortoise which symbolizes the universe and is supposed to be imperishable. Robert Kroetsch, sun hat askew, arms folded, listened to Mr. Wang explain how the emperors were buried facing south, the imperial direction, so that they could continue their rule after death. Death after all, is only another phase of existence. Suzanne was reflected in the large gold urns that are actually fire extinguishers, once filled with earth or water. There goes Gary, bounding up steps next to the marble slabs of clouds, dragons, phoenixes, and flaming pearls that only an emperor once could see. No one can possibly go through this place without being changed, for being changed is part of the process.

Incongruously, lectures in English, Spanish and French boomed across the courtyards from hidden loudspeakers. This was another side of China, the tourism side. Japanese tour guides bellowed out highlights to their groups through orange bullhorns. Like a symphony, the Forbidden City built upwards on a crescendo. Then, just when it seemed my head would explode from the heat, and the expanding gold roofs, we entered a small grotto. A fountain. Zen stones. We walked past a perfect gold elephant sitting on its haunches, a small park with a gazebo where families rested on benches. Then, through a final archway, past the tour buses, on a hill in the distance, made from the dirt excavated from the moat, a final palace, framed by two pagodas. The hill, a coda, was set at the north end of the Forbidden City to deflect yin or evil spirits from that direction, and the small palace on top, the last lingering note following the tumultuous conclusion of a symphony.

Kroetsch tells me he wrote in his journal. "Walked through the Forbidden City today. Fucking incredible."

Following a banquet, we applauded not the chef, but the duck. The strength of a landscape painting was not always in the delicate brush strokes that suggests the mountain, but in the foam and froth of a waterfall created by a complete absence of paint. Old men freshened their breath with metal tongue scrapers. The Chinese dragons are friendly beasts, but anyone touching their scales can die. Even as I made notes, or tried to order random jottings, I felt myself succumbing to the natural rhythm of China.

Not that China was always so complex in meaning. 800 million Chinese live simple rural lives. The hard facts of living off the land, of surviving droughts by eating potato leaves and rice hulls. Farmers took pigs to market. Herded a flock of ducks with long poles. Fishermen floated down river on rafts with their cormorants. Perhaps Chinese farmers, as we did, commented on the green irridescence of a rice paddy after a rain. Set out their wicker baskets of giant leeks which caught the sunlight. Kids scampered about in open-bottomed pants, a practical way of solving the diaper shortage. Adele loved this.

And always the bicycles. My first morning in China, I saw what must have been a million Chinese going to work, the tires of their Phoenix, or Flying Pigeon brand bicyles buzzing, and not one it seemed, had gears or lights. Yet several were loaded down with crates, or pipes, or sugarcane. Policemen in white jackets with red epaulets stood on intersection platforms under umbrellas futilely directing traffic which ignored them.

At those times, I saw the Chinese as they see themselves in international propaganda magazines like *China Pictorial.* In a field, cheerful women, their heads shielded by conical straw hats, pumped their feet up and down on rice hoppers fed by other women. The will of the people launched ships, and happy brigades increased production in factories and communes. Naturalists quietly investigated the habits of giant pandas in their northern bamboo forests. In the south, artists mastered the esoteric art of eglomisé, or reverse glass painting. Using a microscopic paint brush on a curved wire, they painted detailed landscape scenes on the inside of a small snuff bottle.

But with change comes confusion. China can shift its meanings as quickly as a road map held upside down. I was so aware of the terrible China of the police state. I saw the statues defaced by the Red Guard. Saw how our translator could not join us in our room for a drink, and had to sign himself into a hotel. I heard of pickpockets, street crime, the disgusting poverty that train travellers see from their window. The politics of China would require a lifetime to penetrate. And the transformations within me continued. Perhaps not as fast as the Chinese can say of their paintings: "The transformation from ink to fish took place in a twinkling." But it was, indeed, happening.

Kroetsch said that the trip, in its vastness and catalogue of details, its processes, and perspectives, reminded him of a long poem. "A long poem," Adele added, "by the people who were masters of the short poem." Adele's own transformation took place in Heavenly Lake, where she swam in a red bathing suit. Though it was only a small reservoir behind a dam in the hills of southern China, it was her place of enlightenment. As characters in this long poem, we went from event to event, open to everything, breaking down assumptions about China, and about each other. The experience came at us, minute by minute.

Line by line.
Rilke said, *You must change your life.*
In China, we did.

Evidence of transformations, clues, abounded in the Friendship stores, where we zealously shopped after each visit to a monument. Buffalo horns were turned into a pair of delicate crayfish. The thick middle section of an elephant's tusk was carved into as many as twenty ivory balls inside each other, nineteen of them moving separately, and the outer one traditionally carved with nine dragons. Beets and carrots were carved into flowers. One of the oddest things in China was how *anything* could be *something* else. Metaphors existed everywhere. The poetic genius of the Chinese lies in their ability to spontaneously find the metaphor.

Outside most buildings in China are usually found a pair of bronze and porcelain Buddhist Dogs of Fo. They look like lions and represent yin and yang. One always holds a pearl under his foot, and to lose this pearl, which averts floods, dust storms, fires, and disturbances within a city, could cost the Fo Dog his life. Every image honoured story, honoured narrative, honoured language.

As guests of a writers' association, we exchanged many ideas about language and literature. We had five key meetings, and after each, I was impressed by the respect the Chinese have for words. The calligraphers can write "prosperity" or "longevity" one hundred different ways. Sometimes a dot is put inside a word to give it more power. As an editor in Canada, I had not yet fully appreciated the power of language. But the Chinese began it all several thousand years ago. In ancient ceremonies, the priests inserted hot irons into the shin bones of oxen, or the empty shells of tortoises. The cracks were read. They developed into pictograms, and eventually ideograms. Confucius called brush, ink block, ink slab, and paper the Four Treasures of the room of literature. That was a learning experience for me. The writer had to honour his ancient craft. Like a zen archer, the writer in China, however, had to do it correctly the first time. He could not go back to fill in. He had to be sure of his move. Each character had to fill an imaginary square, suggest life and movement; the character needed both a flowing rhythm, and a feeling of suspended motion. Like a small painting. Like this story.

I thought about this often in China. As Canadian writers, we were forging our own forms. Yet how permanent are they? In a museum in Xian, we saw a "forest of stelae", stone tablets with poems carved on them. Set around the classic teaching of Confucius, some of these tablets are over ten feet high. Madame Fan claimed the museum held 10,000 tablets. For myself as an editor, working on a small literary magazine in Canada suggests fragility, impermanence, a feeling my work is only as good as the past issue. Presenting poetry on stone suggests the greatest of respect for poetry. To be a Canadian writer in China was a humbling reminder of the youth of our literature. Of my contributions to it. As Kroetsch said, "It's all in the failure."

Ancient Chinese poetry impressed me with its quiet beauty, but contemporary Chinese writing, as I discovered it firsthand, was somewhat disappointing. Despite the alertness of the fiction writers, poets, editors, and critics we met, I was saddened by the limitations I perceived in their work. I have since read a few good anthologies, and have come to mixed conclusions. The writers we talked to in Beijing, Xian, and Guangzchou had political pressures put upon them. They were sent to the soldiers, farmers, and workers with their creative energies to serve the aims of socialism. Given that their creative work is fueled by historical forces, I saw it as a mixture of self-sacrifice, utopian ideals, and naive optimism. Traditional literature, as we heard over and over again, contains an intense urge to get something done. Fight the enemy, often the Japanese of the 1940s, move the mountain, build the power dam. The poems read to us in China celebrated the collective life, and emphasized the state myth. The Chinese poets we met wanted to give inspiration to their fellowmen. Their poems were often enthusiastic, but simple, glorifying the group struggle to create the myth of modern China.

Yet the pain they had endured was immense. Nearly all the

writers we met had been "sent into the country" for rehabilitation. The novelists we talked to were still bitter about the crisis of the Cultural Revolution. The Gang of Four had scuttled the policy of letting "one hundred flowers bloom." Now we had to believe the novelist, Mr. Lee Jun, when he told us, "Now the Chinese people speak from their hearts. Their writing is the embodiment of the thinking and feeling of the people. Now it is full of life."

Yet I felt some confusion in literary China. Work that expressed the genuine emotions of the common people lacked an aesthetic polish. While I was more than impressed to hear that the Chinese have over 180 literary magazines, with circulations from 100,000 to over one million (and the Chinese were equally amazed to hear that we would even bother to start the presses for our literary magazines, with circulations of a thousand or less), I was also aware of the immense audience that the Chinese have to serve. The pressure to please that many readers must be enormous. Not only do dams, poultry, and produce have to increase in production, so must poetry. Teams of cultural workers were sent to farms, factory areas, and frontiers to encourage stories, verses, and the publication of poems. This movement swept China in the 1960s, was submerged in the 1970s, and when the generals changed their minds, re-emerged in the 1980s. Yet the most poetic moment for me was during a performance of the Peking Opera, when the star did a slow backbend while sipping a cup of wine held between his teeth.

But I think even the Chinese know the limits upon their poetry. They can only get so much poetic credibility when a farmer, labourer, and folk singer compose a panegyric in honour of a good harvest, the new pipeline, or the hydro-electric dam. I think this explains why we were invited. The Chinese are seeking — timidly — new forms and ideas. Hadn't Chinese poetry in this century been influenced by John Dewey, the French Symbolists, the English Romantics, the Indian mystic Tagore? Why not us? A recent special issue of the Peking journal, *Foreign Literature*, featured Canadian writing by Gilles Vigneault, Marcel Dubé, George Ryga, Robert Kroetsch,

Margaret Laurence, Morley Callaghan, Sinclair Ross, and Northrop Frye. This group of writers from Canada could very well be a major influence on future Chinese literature.

Stephen Leacock is still popular, and Mr. Bi told us he first became acquainted with Canadian writers through the poems of Dr. Norman Bethune, written around 1938 on the Long March.

A poet in Xian was interested in landscape poetry. He wanted to know about the Klondike Gold Rush, and logging in Canada. Later, Patrick asked if China has a literature of despair. Mr. Lee Jun, a novelist, replied: "When I was released from prison, my wife was in tears. I asked her if she was happy. She said she was happier than living in a dream. Happier now than when we were dreaming, could be the case of Chinese writers."

Miss Zhang Kankan, at 29, the youngest of the Chinese writers we met, said Chinese writers had missed a decade of writing because of the Cultural Revolution. To Patrick she said, "We also write of tragedy in real life. We encourage these works to give hope because there is hope in life. Without that ideal, we couldn't overthrow the Gang of Four. But we also publish sad stories which might have some influence. When people look back on their suffering, it might give others some hope. China is an old country, and a stubborn one."

Patrick answered his own question a day later in his speech: "By writing of despair, the world is changed. Writers say we will never allow this to happen again. A literature based only on hope can also be a lie."

☯

In the centre of my map of China is Xian. We fly the 1,200 miles from Beijing in an old turboprop with rattling propellors. No air conditioning, despite intense summer heat. Instead, we are given paper fans. "Keep flapping," Kroetsch quips. "This is how we'll get there."

We arrive, as usual, late at night and are met by a small delegation of writers. A poet apoligizes for our short stay in

Xian, but due to a great number of visitors to the ancient capital of China, there is a lack of hotel space. Xian, until 1978 completely off limits to visitors, is now one of the most visited places in China. Adele is so excited she proposes touring in the dark.

Xian is an ancient place. At times I feel as if I am T.S. Eliot's Chinese vase in the Four Quartets, with time past, time present, and time future streaming past my ears. I am being pulled through the tonnage of civilization back to the beginning of time. I lose all sense of a place of departure, and am proceeding towards a destination whose only wisdom can be humility. Xian has been occupied by mankind for 500,000 years. Neolithic man lived here. And millenia after that, the Chinese nation began. A dozen dynasties have had Xian as their capital. The first emperor of China, under the name Shih Huang Ti (221-210 B.C.), who began the Ch'in dynasty which gave China its name, is buried here. He is buried in an unexcavated mausoleum, which legend notes, contains a river of mercury and as many pearls in the ceiling as stars in the night sky. Legend also notes he was a cruel emperor. Feeling that tradition hindered new ideas, he burned all the books. He sent scholars to join the slave labourers building his Great Wall. But the legend makes no mention of the terracotta army.

On those dusty plains, the centre of China, we move in slow motion in the sweltering heat. Here, in a field under a quonset hut, we see the most spectacular archeological find of the twentieth century, the standing army of the emperor Ch'in. I view this place, trembling, the hairs on my neck on end. Peasants, digging a well around the burial mound, uncovered life-sized terracotta figures of soldiers, each different, each apparently modelled from life. At least 6,000 figures have been discovered in eleven long corridors. Then, at each cardinal point of the compass, fragments of three more armies were discovered. Some of these figures were crushed by a collapsing roof. Arms, legs, bits of heads poked through the reddish earth at odd angles. The army included life-sized horses pulling chariots which have long ago disintegrated into the earth.

I will go on unearthing that army, and feel as terrified as the peasants who first thought the figures were ghosts. Traces of paint remain on them. In their lifelike poses, the archers, spearmen, charioteers, and kung fu masters inspire an unnatural fear. I feel that cold recollection of something half forgotten, or something quickly seen from the corner of my eye, something half felt. In unearthing that army, I find an army in myself. A quick reminder of that time not two weeks ago in the hotel courtyard where I watched tai chi performed. What else lies under this earth? The dirt falls on these soldiers, on their small eyelids, on the hands of clay, the precise folds of their terracotta garments. No longer can we take the earth for granted when an army marches beneath us. What kind of imagination would a 27 year old emperor have to have, to want to surround himself for all eternity with a spectacle like this. What traces of traces, what fragments of fragments will remain of my work?

Sipping tea later, under cooling fans in a room hot as a cook stove, we calmly discuss the site and the problems of archeology in China. The immense costs to a poor country, the extremes of hot and cold in central China, the problems of preserving archeological treasures. Air entering airtight tombs after several centuries turns linen, wood, fabric, plaster, and bodies to dust.

None of us can discuss the larger implications of Xian. Instead, we laugh, tell jokes, ask intelligent questions about the site. But when we leave, I look back. The temperature in the late afternoon is over 100 degrees. There, by the burial mound, alone between earth and sky, I see an old farmer with a white beard, no hat, and a shirt as dusty as the field he crossed. I see myself.